A Study

of the Assimilation and

Substitution in Arabic

Joyce Åkesson

Pallas Athena

Lund

2010

A Study of the Assimilation and Substitution in Arabic

2010 Pallas Athena Distribution, Skarpskyttevägen 10 A, 226 42 Lund, Sweden.

Book design by Joyce Åkesson

ISBN: 978-91-977641-6-2

PRINTED IN THE UNITED STATES OF AMERICA

ALSO BY JOYCE ÅKESSON

Majnūn Leyla: Poems about Passion, Pallas Athena Distribution, December 2009.

The Invitation, Pallas Athena Distribution, July 2009.

Love's Thrilling Dimensions, Pallas Athena Distribution, February 2009.

The Essentials of the Class of the Strong Verb in Arabic, Pallas Athena Distribution, January 2010

The Complexity of the Irregular Verbal and Nominal Forms & the Phonological Changes in Arabic, Pallas Athena Distribution, April 2009.

Arabic Morphology and Phonology: Based on the Marāḥ al-Arwāḥ by Aḥmad b. ᶜAlī b. Masᶜūd, Studies in Semitic Languages and Linguistics, Brill Academic Publishers, July 2001.

Aḥmad B. ᶜAlī B. Masᶜūd on Arabic Morphology, Marāḥ al-Arwāḥ: Part 1: The Strong Verb, Studia Orientalia Lundensia, Vol. 4, Brill Academic Publishers, October 1990.

CONTENTS

PREFACE XV

1. The Assimilation 1

1.1. The assimilation in the pronunciation and in the writing 2

1.2. The points of articulation and some of the characters of the segments that lead to the assimilation 3

1.2.1. The segments' common and neighbouring points of articulation: 3

1.2.2. Some of the segments' characters: 5

1.3. The sequences of two identical segments: cases in which the assimilation is or is not carried out 6

1.3.1. The sequence of two identical segments of which the 1st is vowelless and the 2nd vowelled: the necessity of the assimilation: 7

1.3.1.1. The assimilation that is carried out in one word: 8

1.3.1.2. The assimilation that is carried out in two words following each other: 8

1.3.2. The sequence of two identical segments which are both vowelled: the assimilation, except in some anomalous cases: 9

1.3.2.1. The assimilation that is carried out in one word 10

1- Cases in which the 1st of the identical segments is preceded by a fatḥa: 10

2- Cases in which the 1st of the identical segments is preceded by a vowelless segment: 11

1.3.2.2. Cases in which the assimilation is not carried out in one word: 12

1.3.2.2.1. An anomalous case: *ḥayiya* 13

1.3.2.2.2. The coordinatives and some special measures: 14

1.3.2.3. The assimilation that is carried out in two words following each other: 16

1- The *b's* assimilation to the *b:* 17

2- The *ḥ's* assimilation to the *ḥ:* 17

3- The *r's* assimilation to the *r:* 17

4- The *ᶜ's* assimilation to the *ᶜ:* 18

5- The *ġ's* assimilation to the *ġ:* 18

6- The *f's* assimilation to the *f:* 18

7- The *q's* assimilation to the *q:* 18

8- The *k's* assimilation to the *k:* 19

9- The *m's* assimilation to the *m:* 19

10- The *h's* assimilation to the *h:* 19

11- The *y's* assimilation to the *y:* 20

12- The *w's* assimilation to the *w:* 20

1.3.3. The sequence of two identical segments of which the 1st is vowelled and the 2nd vowelless: the prohibition of the assimilation. The assimilation in some anomalous cases. The elision of one of the identical segments. The substitution of one of the identical segments by a yāᵓ: 20

1- The prohibition of the assimilation: 21

2- The assimilation in some anomalous cases: 22

3- The elision of one of the identical segments: 23

4- The substitution of one of the identical segments by a *y:* 26

1.4. The sequence of two different segments: cases in which the assimilation is or is not carried out 28

1.4.1. The sequence of two different segments of which the 1st is vowelless and the 2nd is vowelled: the assimilation: 28

1.4.1.1. The assimilation that is carried out from the 1st vowelless segment to a 2nd different vowelled segment in one word: 29

1- The assimilation of the vowelless *l*- of the article *al*- to the vowelled solar segment that begins a noun: 29

2- The assimilation of the 3rd radical *d* in verbs that occur in the perfect, to the vowelled suffixed pronoun of the agent that begins with the *t:* 30

3. The assimilation that is carried out between the vowelled infixed *t* of Form VIII of the perfect *ᵓiftaᶜala* and the 1st vowelless radical preceding it: 31

1.4.1.1.3.1. Cases in which the 1st vowelless radical is assimilated to the infixed vowelled *t* of Form VIII of the perfect *ᵓiftaᶜala:* 31

1- The assimilation of the 1st radical vowelless *ᵓ* to the vowelled infixed t of Form VIII *ᵓiftaᶜala:* 32

2- The assimilation of the 1st radical vowelless *t* to the vowelled infixed *t* of Form VIII *ᵓiftaᶜala:* 33

3- The assimilation between the 1st radical vowelless *ṯ* and the vowelled infixed t of Form VIII *ᵓiftaᶜala:* 33

4- The assimilation of the 1st radical vowelless *w* to the vowelled infixed *t* of Form VIII *ᵓiftaᶜala:* 33

5- The assimilation of the 1st radical vowelless *y* to the vowelled infixed *t* of Form VIII *ᵓiftaᶜala:* 34

1.4.1.1.3.2. Cases in which the infixed vowelled *t* of Form VIII of the perfect *ᵓiftaᶜala* is assimilated to the 1st vowelless radical preceding it: 34

8- The assimilation of the vowelled prefixed *t* of Form V *tafa^{cc}ala* or Form VI *taf(a)ā^{c}ala* to the 1st vowelled radical *ṣ* following it: 51

9- The assimilation of the vowelled prefixed *t* of Form V *tafa^{cc}ala* or Form VI *taf(a)ā^{c}ala* to the 1st vowelled radical *ḍ* following it: 52

10- The assimilation of the vowelled prefixed *t* of Form V *tafa^{cc}ala* or Form VI *taf(a)ā^{c}ala* to the 1st vowelled radical *ṭ* following it: 52

11- The assimilation of the vowelled prefixed *t* of Form V *tafa^{cc}ala* or Form VI *taf(a)ā^{c}ala* to the 1st vowelled radical *ẓ* following it: 53

1.4.2.1.2. The assimilation of the infixed vowelled *t* of the imperfect of Form VIII *yafta^{c}ilu* to the vowelled 2nd radical: 53

1- The assimilation of the vowelled infixed *t* of Form VIII of the imperfect *yafta^{c}ilu* to the 2nd vowelled radical *t* following it in the imperfect: 54

2- The assimilation of the vowelled infixed *t* of Form VIII of the imperfect *yafta^{c}ilu* to the 2nd vowelled radical *d* following it: 55

3- The assimilation of the vowelled infixed *t* of Form VIII of the imperfect *yafta^{c}ilu* to the vowelled 2nd radical *ḏ* following it: 55

4- The assimilation of the vowelled infixed *t* of Form VIII of the imperfect *yafta^{c}ilu* to the vowelled 2nd radical *z* following it: 56

5- The assimilation of the vowelled infixed *t* of Form VIII of the imperfect *yaftaᶜilu* to the vowelled 2nd radical *s* following it: 56

6- The assimilation of the vowelled infixed *t* of Form VIII of the imperfect *yaftaᶜilu* to the vowelled 2nd radical *ṣ* following it: 57

7- The assimilation of the vowelled infixed *t* of Form VIII of the imperfect *yaftaᶜilu* to the vowelled 2nd radical *ḍ* following it: 58

8- The assimilation of the vowelled infixed *t* of Form VIII of the imperfect *yaftaᶜilu* to the vowelled 2nd radical *ṭ* following it: 58

9- The assimilation of the vowelled infixed *t* of Form VIII of the imperfect *yaftaᶜilu* to the *ẓ* following it: 59

1.4.2.2. The assimilation that is carried out from the 1st vowelled segment to a 2nd vowelled segment in two words following each other: 59

1- The *b's* assimilation to 59

2- The *ṯ's* assimilation to: 60

3- The *ṯ's* assimilation to: 61

4- The *ǧ's* assimilation to: 61

5- The *ḥ's* assimilation to: 62

6- The *d's* assimilation to: 62

7- The *ḏ's* assimilation to: 63

8- The *r's* assimilation to: 63

9- The *s's* assimilation to: 64

10- The *š's* assimilation to: 64

11- The *ḍ's* assimilation to: 64

12- The *f's* assimilation to: 64

13- The *q's* assimilation to: 65

14- The *k's* assimilation to: 65

15- The *l's* assimilation to: 65

16- The *m's* assimilation to: 66

17- The *n's* assimilation to: 66

18- The *h's* assimilation to: 66

2. THE SUBSTITUTION 67

2.1. The segments of substitution 67

2.1.1. The substitution of the hamza 68

2.1.1.1. The substitution of the hamza for the alif of feminization, the *ā (alif maqṣūra):* 68

2.1.1.2. The substitution of the hamza for the *w:* 69

1- The hamza vowelled by a fatḥa: 69

2- The hamza vowelled by a ḍamma: 70

3- The hamza vowelled by a kasra: 71

2.1.1.3. The substitution of the hamza for the *y:* 72

1- The hamza vowelled by a fatḥa: 72

2- The hamza vowelled by a kasra: 73

2.1.1.4. The substitution of the hamza for the *h:* 73

2.1.1.5. The substitution of the hamza for the *ā:* 74

2.1.1.6. The substitution of the hamza for the *ᶜ:* 75

2.1.2. The substitution of the *s* 76

2.1.2.1. The substitution of the *s* for the *t:* 76

2.1.3. The substitution of the *t* 77

2.1.3.1. The substitution of the *t* for the *w:* 77

2.1.3.2. The substitution of the *t* for the *y:* 78

2.1.3.3. The substitution of the *t* for the *d* and the *s:* 79

2.1.3.4. The substitution of the *t* for the *ṣ:* 80

2.1.3.5. The substitution of the *t* for the *b:* 80

2.1.4. The substitution of the *n* 81

2.1.4.1. The substitution of the *n* for the *w:* 81

2.1.4.2. The substitution of the *n* for the *l:* 81

2.1.5. The substitution of the *ǧ* 82

2.1.5.1. The substitution of the *ǧ* for the *y:* 82

2.1.6. The substitution of the *d* 83

2.1.6.1. The substitution of the *d* for the *t:* 84

2.1.7. The substitution of the *h* 84

2.1.7.1. The substitution of the *h* for the hamza: 84

2.1.7.2. The substitution of the *h* for the *ā:* 85

2.1.7.3. The substitution of the *h* for the *y:* 86

2.1.7.4. The substitution of the *h* for the *t:* 86

2.1.8. The substitution of the *y* 87

2.1.8.1. The substitution of the *ī* for the *ā:* 87

2.1.8.2. The substitution of the *y* for the *w:* 88

2.1.8.3. The substitution of the *y* for the hamza: 90

2.1.8.4. The substitution of the *y* for one of the doubled segments in the doubled verb: 90

2.1.8.5. The substitution of the *y* for the *n:* 90

2.1.8.6. The substitution of the *ī* for the ᶜ: 91

2.1.8.7. The substitution of the *y* for the *t:* 92

2.1.8.8. The substitution of the *y* for the *b:* 93

2.1.8.9. The substitution of the *y* for the *s:* 93

2.1.8.10. The substitution of the *y* for the *ṯ:* 94

2.1.9. The substitution of the *w* 95

2.1.9.1. The substitution of the *w* for the *ā:* 95

2.1.9.2. The substitution of the *w* for the *y:* 96

2.1.9.3. The substitution of the *w* for the hamza: 97

2.1.10. The substitution of the *m* 97

2.1.10.1. The substitution of the *m* for the *w:* 97

2.1.10.2. The substitution of the *m* for the *l:* 98

2.1.10.3. The substitution of the *m* for the *n:* 99

2.1.10.4. The substitution of the *m* for the *b:* 100

2.1.11. The substitution of the *ṣ* 100

2.1.11.1. The substitution of the *ṣ* for the *s* 100

2.1.12. The substitution of the *ā* 101

2.1.12.1. The substitution of the *ā* for the *w:* 101

2.1.12.2. The substitution of the *ā* for the *y:* 102

2.1.12.3. The substitution of the *ā* for the hamza: 102

2.1.13. The substitution of the *l* 102

2.1.13.1. The substitution of the *l* for the *n:* 103

2.1.13.2. The substitution of the *l* for the *ḍ:* 103

2.1.14. The substitution of the *z* 104

2.1.14.1. The substitution of the *z* for the *s:* 104

2.1.14.2. The substitution of the *z* for the *ṣ:* 105

2.1.15. The substitution of the *ṭ* 105

2.1.15.1. The substitution of the *ṭ* for the *t:* 106

3. Bibliography 109

3.1. Primary sources 109

3.2. Secondary sources 113

4. Index of Qurʾanic quotations   117

5. Index of verses   121

6. Index of names   123

PREFACE

This work is a comprehensive study of two well-known phonological changes in Arabic: the assimilation and the substitution.

The assimilation involves the incorporation of a certain segment into an adjacent one in such a manner that they both form a doubled segment. The segments can either be identical or different. This phenomenon occurs usually in the doubled verbs and their forms and in some cases of perfects of Form V, VI and VIII. It also occurs in some other more unusual cases as in two words following each other.

The substitution involves the replacement of a segment for another different one. It occurs if there is in the word a combination of two segments which is deemed as heavy, or if both these segments' points of articulation are close to each other or if they are akin in character. Other more unusual reasons relate to the peculiarity of a dialectal variant, to a verse's metrical exigency or to the exigency of the pause.

This book explores in detail many various cases in which these changes are possible, necessary or forbidden.

The phonological elements, the theoretical discussions and the coverage of the different works from the 8th century until our days, offer a thorough and accessible study for both the students and researchers of Arabic.

1. THE ASSIMILATION

The assimilation is termed as *ʾidġām* or *ʾiddiġām*. It involves a sequence of two identical segments, e.g. *maddun* (مدّ) "an extension" (for discussions see par. 1.3.), or of two different segments originating from one common point of articulation or from two close points of articulation, e.g. الرَّحْمٰن *al-Raḥmān* "the Merciful" (for discussions see par. 1.4).

It can be carried out in one word e.g. *maddun* or in two words following each other, e.g. *la-ḏaha(b) bbi-samᶜihim* (لَذَهَب بِّسَمْعِهِم) (for discussions see par. 1.3.2.3.).

Furthermore it differs in the pronunciation and in the writing, e.g *"ar-Raḥmān"* pronounced as so and written *al-Raḥmān* الرَّحْمٰن (cf. 1.1.).

The reason why the assimilation is carried out is the dislike of repeating twice the same segment or of pronouncing two segments that are close to each other in the point of articulation. On the basis that the assimilation can be carried out between segments that are different, the segments' points of articulation and characters shall be introduced (cf. 1.2.).

Hence the theories concerning the assimilation or the lack of assimilation in a few sequences that are formed of two identical or different segments are presented and analyzed in this study.

1.1. The assimilation in the pronunciation and in the writing

There is a difference in the pronunciation and in the written representation of a word in which an assimilation is carried out.

In examples in which two identical segments are assimilated, e.g. *madda,* two dāls are uttered in the pronunciation, namely *mad-da,* of which the first *d* is vowelless and the second one vowelled: مَدْدَ. In the writing however, one *d* is written with a šadda over it: مَدَّ.

In examples of nouns beginning with one of the "solar segments" to which the *l-* of the definite article *al-* is assimilated to (for discussions see par. 1.4.1.1.1.), the nouns are pronounced with the doubling of the solar segment and written with both the *l-* of the article and the solar segment given the *šadda.* An example is *"ar-Raḥmān"* pronounced with a double *r* indicating the assimilation of the *l-* to the *r,* and written *al-Raḥmān* الرَّحْمٰن "the Merciful" with the *l* and with the *r* that carries the *šadda.*

1.2. The points of articulation and some of the characters of the segments that lead to the assimilation

An assimilation between two different segments requires that these segments originate either from a common point of articulation or from close points of articulation. There should as well exist an akinity in character between both these segments or that a segment exhibits a strength of character in relation to the other, which would explain why the assimilation is carried out to it.

1.2.1. The segments' common and neighbouring points of articulation:

Among the first grammarians who gave a detailed description of the segments' points of articulation and characters, Sībawaihi, II, 452-455 can be mentioned. The following segments have common or neighbouring points of articulation (cf. also Versteegh, *Language* 20).

- The ᵓ, *h,* and *ā* originate from "the farthest part of the throat" and the *ġ* and *ḫ* from "the nearest part of the throat". They are characterized as laryngals.

- The ᶜ and *ḥ* originate from "the middle of the throat". They are characterized as pharyngals.

- The *q* originates from "the farthest part of the tongue, and the part of the upper palate above it". The *k* is "lower than the *q* from the next parts of the tongue and palate towards the upper palate". They are characterized as post-palatals.

- The *ǧ, š* and *y* originate from "the middle of the tongue, and from the middle part of the upper palate". They are characterized as pre-palatals.

- The *ṭ, d* and the *t* originate from "the tip of the tongue and the roots of the two upper central incissors". The *ḍ* originates from "the first part of the side of the tongue, and the molars below (on the left or right side)". They are characterized as alveolars.

- The *l* originates from "between the nearest part of the side of the tongue, to the end of its tip, and the part of the upper palate next to it, a little above the premolar, canine, lateral incisor, and central incisor".

- The *ṣ, z* and *s* originate from "the part that is between the tip of the tongue and the tops of the two upper central incissors". The *n* is from the tip of the tongue and the parts over the incissors". They are characterized as dentals.

- The *ẓ*, *ḏ* and *ṯ* originate from "the tip of the tongue and the edges of the two upper central incisors". They are characterized as interdentals.

- The *f* originates from "the inside of the lower lip and the edges of the two upper central incisors". The *b*, *m* and *w* originate from "what is between the lips". These segments are characterized as labials.

1.2.2. Some of the segments' characters:

Among the most specifying characters of the segments are those of *al-mahmūsa* "surd, low, soft, whispered, voiceless" and of *al-mağhūra* "vocal, loud, clear, sonorous, voiced".

The surd segments are comprised in the sentence *sa-tašḥaṯuka Ḫaṣfah* (cf. for them Zamaḫšarī, 189, Åkesson, *Ibn Masᶜūd* 198: fol. 19a, Howell, IV, fasc. II, 1725). They are: the *s*, *t*, *š*, *ḥ*, *ṯ*, *k*, *ḫ*, *ṣ*, *f* and *h*. Sībawaihi, II, 453 presents them in this order: the *h*, *ḥ*, *ḫ*, *k*, *š*, *s*, *t*, *ṣ*, *ṯ* and *f*. They are weak in the stress laid upon them so that they do not impede the breath that therefore runs on with them.

The voiced segments are comprised in the sentence *ẓillu Qawwin rabaḍun ᵓiḏ ġazā ğundun muṭīᶜun* "the shade of Qaww was a shelter, when an obediant host made a raid" (cf. Howell, IV, fasc. II, 1726). They prevent the breath from running on with them. Sībawaihi, II, 453 presents them in this order: the *ᵓ*, *ā*, *ᶜ*, *ġ*, *q*, *ğ*, *y*, *ḍ*, *l*, *n*, *r*, *ṭ*, *d*, *z*, *ẓ*, *ḏ*, *b*, *m* and *w*.

There are other secondary characters that the segments of these main groups can present (for a detailed presentation of the characters see. Sībawaihi, II, 454-455) as:

- *al-mustaᶜliya* "the elevated", which are comprised in the combination *ṣaṭ ḍaẓ ḫaġaq* (cf. Zamaḫšarī, 190, Åkesson, *Ibn Masᶜūd* 198: fol. 19b), namely the *ṣ, ṭ, ḍ, ẓ, ḫ, ġ* and *q*. The first four segments, namely the *ṣ, ṭ, ḍ* and *ẓ* are recognized as *al-muṭbaqa* "the covered" (cf. Sībawaihi, II, 455, Åkesson, *Ibn Masᶜūd* 198: fol. 19b). Their point of articulation is covered by the upper palate. The three remaining segments, namely the *ḫ, ġ* and *q* do not present any covering.

- *al-munḫafiḍa* "the depressed segments" which are contrary to the elevated (cf. Zamaḫšarī, 190, Howell, IV, fasc. II, 1729-1731).

- *al-ṣafīr* "sibilant" which are the three segments: the *ṣ, z* and *s*, which make a whistling.

1.3. The sequences of two identical segments: cases in which the assimilation is or is not carried out

The sequences of two identical segments can occur in one word or in two words following each other. In the case of the assimilation which is carried out between two segments belonging to two different words, it is the ultimate segment of the first word that can be assimilated to the initial segment of the second word (for such cases see Sībawaihi, II, 455 sqq.,

Zamaḫšarī, 191 sqq., Roman, *Étude I,* 390-427, Wright, I, 15-16). This assimilation is not as usual as the assimilation that is carried out in one word, and can be seen as belonging to the rarities.

The following sequences can be mentioned:

1.3.1. the sequence of two identical segments of which the 1st is vowelless and the 2nd vowelled: the necessity of the assimilation.

1.3.2. the sequence of two identical segments which are both vowelled: the assimilation, except in some anomalous cases.

1.3.3. the sequence of two identical segments of which the 1st is vowelled and the 2nd vowelless: the prohibition of the assimilation. The assimilation in some anomalous cases.

Not all the sequences can result in the assimilation of the 1st segment to the 2nd. It shall be noticed that the most important condition of the assimilation is the vowelling of the 2nd segment.

1.3.1. The sequence of two identical segments of which the 1st is vowelless and the 2nd vowelled: the necessity of the assimilation:

The vowelless state of the 1st segment preceding a vowelled identical segment answers to the condition that makes the assimilation necessary.

This sequence can be found in one word or in two words following each other.

1.3.1.1. The assimilation that is carried out in one word:

An example of such a case is *maddun* (مدّ) "an extension" that is formed according to the pattern *fa^clun,* with two dāls written of which the 1st *d* is vowelless and the 2nd one is vowelled. After the assimilation of the dāls it becomes *maddun* with the doubled *d* referred to in Arabic by the *d* carrying the *šadda:* (مَدٌّ) .

Another example is Form VIII *ᵓittaǧara* "to trade" (cf. Åkesson, *Ibn Masᶜūd* 196: fol. 19a, par. 1.4.1.1.3.1.:2) from *taǧara* with 1st *t* radical. In the base form *ᵓittaǧara,* the 1st vowelless *t* radical is followed by the vowelled *t* infix, the *ta,* of Form VIII *ᵓiftaᶜala,* which necessitates the assimilation of the *t* to the *t*. Hence *ᵓittaǧara* is written with one *t* carrying the *šadda* in Arabic (إتّجَر) as an indication of the assimilation .

1.3.1.2. The assimilation that is carried out in two words following each other:

The assimilation can be carried out from a 1st vowelless segment, which is the last segment of a word, to a 2nd identical vowelled segment that is the initial segment of the word following it.

An example of such a case is *(ʾiḫšaw w(a)āqidan)* (إِخْشَوْ واقدا) "Fear [2nd person of the masc. pl. of the imperative] one who sets fire!" (cf. Sībawaihi, II, 457) in which the 1st *w* is vowelless and the 2nd *w* is vowelled by a fatḥa. The reason of the vowellessness of the 1st *w* is that the verb *ʾiḫšaw* is an imperative in the 2nd person of the masc. pl. with the suffixed pronoun of the masc. pl., the *ū,* vowelless and preceded by a fatḥa which results in *aw*. The example becomes after the assimilation of the vowelless *w* to the vowelled *wa, ʾiḫša(w) ww(a)āqidan* (إِخْشَو وّاقدا) with the 2nd *w* carrying the *šadda* as an indication of the assimilation.

1.3.2. The sequence of two identical segments which are both vowelled: the assimilation, except in some anomalous cases:

The sequence of two identical vowelled segments leads mostly to the assimilation, except in some anomalous cases as the case of *ḥayiya* "to live" (cf. par. 1.3.2.2.1.), in the coordinatives and in somes measures that can be mixed up with other measures (cf. par. 1.3.2.2.2.).

The assimilation can be carried out in one word or in two words, and in the latter case the assimilation is a possibility that pertains to the rarities.

1.3.2.1. The assimilation that is carried out in one word:

The 1st of the two identical segments can be preceded by a fatḥa or by a vowelless segment. In the first case, the 1st segment is assimilated to the 2nd identical segment. In the 2nd case, the vowel of the 1st segment is transferred to the vowelless segment preceding it before that it is assimilated to the identical segment following it.

1- Cases in which the 1st oi the identical segments is preceded by a fatḥa:

a- In examples of doubled verbs in the perfect of Form I of the 3rd persons. In these forms, the vowel of the 2nd radical, which is preceded by a fatḥa, is dropped and the 2nd radical is assimilated to the 3rd. Thus the following forms of the masc. sing.:

sarara	→	*sarra* "he gladdened"
farara	→	*farra* "he escaped"
ᶜaḍiḍa	→	*ᶜaḍḍa* "he bit"
ḥabuba	→	*ḥabba* "he loved"

It can be noted that the following variations occur concerning the verbs *farra* and *ᶜaḍḍa* (for them see Howell, IV, fasc. II, 1699). Asad and some other people say *firra* and *ᶜaḍḍa* by vowelling the 1st radical with a ḍamma, kasra or fatḥa respectively and by assimilating the 2nd radical to the 3rd vowelled by a fatḥa. Kaᶜb and Numair say *firri* and *ᶜaḍḍi* by vowelling the 1st radical with a ḍamma, kasra or fatḥa respectively and by assimilating the 2nd radical to the 3rd radical vowelled with the kasra. Other variants pertaining to their dialect are *firri* and *ᶜaḍḍa* with the alliteration of the vowel of the 1st radical and with the 2nd radical assimilated to the 3rd that is given the same vowel as the 1st radical's vowel.

b- In examples of verbs of Form V *tafaᶜᶜala* or Form VI *taf(a)āᶜala* in which the vowelled prefixed *t* is assimilated to the 1st vowelled radical *t* following it (for discussions see par. 1.4.2.1.1.).

An example is Form V *tatarrasa* "shielded himself" that becomes after the assimilation *ᵓittarasa* (cf. Howell, IV, fasc. II, 1829). The vowelled *t* prefix, i.e. the *ta,* is assimilated to the vowelled 1st radical *t,* i.e. the *ta,* resulting in *ttarasa* and the prosthetic hamza, the *ᵓi,* is then prefixed to prevent beginning the word with a vowelless segment.

2- Cases in which the 1st oi the identical segments is preceded by a vowelless segment:

a- In examples of doubled verbs in the imperfect of Form I. The phonological procedure that is observed is that the vowel of the 2nd radical is not dropped but switched to the 1st vowelless radical preceding it, and the 2nd radical is assimilated to the 3rd. Hence:

yasruru	→	*yasurru* "he gladdens"
yafriru	→	*yafirru* "he escapes"
yaᶜḍadu	→	*yaᶜaḍḍu* "he bites"
yaḥbubu	→	*yaḥubbu* "he loves"

b- In examples of verbs of Form VIII in the imperfect *yaftaᶜilu* in which the vowelled infixed *t* is assimilated to the 2nd vowelled radical *t* following it (for discussions see par. 1.4.2.1.2.).

An example is *yaqtatilu* "to contend among themselves" that becomes after the assimilation *yaqattilu* (cf. Åkesson, *Ibn Masᶜūd* 200: fol. 20b). The vowelled *t* prefix, i.e. the *ta,* is assimilated to the vowelled 2nd radical, i.e. *ti,* after that its fatḥa vowel is shifted to the 1st radical *q*. It can be noted that both variants *yaqattilu* and *yaqittilu* occur (cf. Zamaḫšarī, 195, Howell, IV, fasc. II, 1807).

1.3.2.2. Cases in which the assimilation is not carried out in one word:

The assimilation is mostly not carried out in the case of *ḥayiya* "to live" (cf. par. 1.3.2.2.1.), in the co-ordinatives and in some special measures (cf. 1.3.2.2.2.).

<u>1.3.2.2.1. An anomalous case: ḥayiya</u>

The assimilation is not carried out in some dialectal variants in the doubled verb with two weak radicals *ḥayiya* "to live" (for discussions concerning it see Sībawaihi, II, 430-431, Zamaḫšarī, 187, Ibn ᶜAqīl, II, 588, Åkesson, *Ibn Masᶜūd* 194: fol. 18a, Howell, IV, fasc. I, 1624 sqq., fasc. II, 1693 sqq., Wright, II, 94-95, Vernier, I, 342-343, de Sacy, I, 259-260). In spite of the fact that two vowelled identical segments are combined in it, namely the *yi* and the *ya,* they are not in most cases assimilated together resulting in *ḥayya.* The assimilation is carried out however in some dialectal variants. The reason why some prefer not to assimilate the yāᵓs in the perfect resulting in *ḥayya,* is that they feel obliged by analogy to assimilate them in the imperfect causing the ḍamma to vowel the *y* which is deemed as a heavy combination, i.e. *yaḥayyu* would have to be said instead of *yaḥy(a)ā* with final *ᵓalif maqṣūra.* Those who assimilate in the perfect by saying *ḥayya* consider both yāᵓs as two identical vowelled segments in one word. They avoid however to assimilate in the imperfect because of the implied heavy combination. This means that *yaḥy(a)ā* with final *alif maqṣūra* occurs by all instead of *yaḥayyu.*

Furthermore, the 3rd radical *y* has been dropped by some in the perfect of the 3rd person of the masc. pl., who use *ḥay(u)ū* instead of *ḥayiyū* (cf. Sībawaihi, II, 431, Ibn Manẓūr, II, 1080). *Ḥay(u)ū* occurs in this verse said by an anonymous poet cited by Sībawaihi, II, 431, Ibn Yaᶜīš, X, 116, Ibn Manẓūr, II, 1080, Howell, IV, fasc. I, 1630:

> *"Wa-kunnā ḥasibnāhum fawārisa kahmasi*
> *ḥayū baᶜdamā mātū mina l-dahri ᵓaᶜṣurā".*
> "And we have accounted them to be horsemen of Kahmas [a man from Tamīm celebrated for horsemanship and valour], who after they had died, lived through ages of time".

This elision of the *y* implies that it is considered as unnecessary to the word's structure (cf. Åkesson, *Ibn Masᶜūd* 194: fol. 18a). On the basis that the 2nd segment among two identical segments is not necessary for the structure of the word, it can be understood why the assimilation is not always carried out in the perfect *ḥayiya,* as the condition of the assimilation is that the 2nd segment among the identical segments should be existent in the structure and not submitted to an elision.

1.3.2.2.2. The coordinatives and some special measures:

The assimilation is forbidden in *al-ᵓilḥāqīyāt* "the co-ordinatives", in spite of the vowelling of two identical segments in them. These patterns refer to those words that are rendered quasi-coordinate to other words of which the radicals are greater in number than theirs (cf. Lane, II 3008).

An example is a measure with the repetition of the 3rd consonant of the triliteral in it, e.g. *qardadun* "elevated ground" (cf. Sībawaihi, II, 448, Åkesson, *Ibn Mas^{c}ūd* 194: 17b) from the root *qarida* "it became contracted together", in which the 2nd *d* is added to the form, and no assimilation is to be carried out from the first vowelled *d,* the *da,* to the other vowelled *d,* the *dun,* on account that the word is quasi-coordinate to the measure *fa^{c}lalun* (cf. Lane, II, 2513).

Other examples of measures with the repetition of the 3rd consonant are (cf. Fleish, *Arabe* 75-76):

- *duḫlulun* and *diḫlulun* "intruder" conformable to *fu^{c}lulun* and *fi^{c}lulun* respectively.

- *ḫufdudun* "bat" conformable to *fu^{c}lulun.*

- *^{c}undadun* "retreat" conformable to *fu^{c}lalun.*

- *rimdidun* “ashes” conformable to *fi^{c}lilun.*

It can be remarked that some measures with this repetition of the 3rd consonant have the first vowel short and the second one lengthened, e.g. *zilzālun* “earthquake” conformable to *fi^{c}lālun, siktītun* “very silent” conformabele to *fi^{c}līlun, ḥulbūbun* “very black” conformable to *fu^{c}lūlun* and *baynūnatun* “to be separated” “conformable to *fa^{c}lūlatun.*

The assimilation is as well forbidden in some words that are formed according to special measures (cf. Sībawaihi, II, 445-446, Åkesson, *Ibn Mas^{c}ūd* 194: fol. 18a) as *fa^{c}ilun, fu^{c}ulun, fu^{c}alun* and *fa^{c}alun,* so that they are not mixed up with other words in which the assimilation is carried out. Some examples are:

- *ṣakikun* "the colliding of the knees in running" formed according to *fa^{c}ilun* to avoid mixing it up with *ṣakkun* "a written acknowledgement of a debt".

- *sururun* "bedsteads" formed according to *fu^{c}ulun* to avoid mixing it up with *surrun* "the navel- string of a child". Sībawaihi, II, 446 remarks however that some said *surrun* instead of it and alleviated.

- *ğudadun* "the stripes that are on the back of the ass" formed according to *fu^{c}alun* to avoid mixing it up with *ğuddun* "a part of the river near the land".

- *ṭalalun* "the remains of a dwelling or house" formed according to *fa^{c}alun* to avoid mixing it up with *ṭallun* "weak rain".

1.3.2.3. The assimilation that is carried out in two words following each other:

The assimilation can be carried out from a 1st vowelled segment, which is the 1st segment of a word, to a 2nd identical vowelled segment that is the initial segment of the word following it. This assimilation occurs in a few readings of the suras from the Qur^{ɔ}an, but not only in them. The following cases can be presented:

1- The b's assimilation to the b:

An example of such a case is the assimilation of the bā'’s in a reading of the sur. 2: 19 *(la-ḏahaba bi-samᶜihim)* that becomes *la-ḏaha(b) bbi-samᶜihim* (لَذَهَ بِّسَمْعِهِم) "He would take away their faculty of hearing", read so by Abū ᶜAmr (cf. Zamaḫšarī, 195, Ibn Yaᶜīš, X, 147) with the fatḥa of the 1st *b,* the *ba,* elided and the šadda given to the 2nd *b* as an indication of the assimilation. An analysis of *la-ḏahaba bi-samᶜihim* before that the assimilation of the bā'ˀs is carried out in it, shows that the first *b* which is the 3rd radical of *ḏahaba,* is vowelled by a fatḥa that is the marker of the undeclinable perfect and the 2nd *b* which is the 1st segment of the word following it, is vowelled by the kasra as it is the preposition *bi.*

Another example is a reading of the sur. 3: 151 *(al-ruᶜ(b) bbi-mā)* "Terror [into the hearts of the Unbelievers], for that", read so by Abū ᶜAmr (cf. Ibn ᶜUṣfūr, II, 719).

2- The ḥ's assimilation to the ḥ:

An example is a reading of the sur. 2: 235 *(ᶜuqdata l-nikā(ḥ) ḥḥattā)* "The tie of marriage till" (cf. Ibn Yaᶜīš, X, 137).

3- The r's assimilation to the r:

An example is a reading of the sur. 7: 77 *(wa-ᶜataw ᶜan ˀam(r) rrabbihim)* "And insolently defied the order of their

Lord" and the sur. 19: 2 *(ḏik(r) rraḥmati)* "(This is) a recital of the Mercy", read so by Abū ᶜAmr (cf. Ibn ᶜUṣfūr, II, 722).

4- The ᶜ's assimilation to the ᶜ:

An example is a reading of the sur. 2: 255 *(man ḏā l-laḏī yašfa(ᶜ) ᶜᶜindahu)* "Who is there can intercede in His presence" (cf. Zamaḫšarī, 192, Ibn Yaᶜīš, X, 136).

5- The ġ's assimilation to the ġ:

An example is a reading of the sur. 3: 85 *(wa-man yabta(ġ) ġġayra l-ᵓislāmi dīnan)* "If anyone desires a religion other than Islam (submission to God)" (cf. Zamaḫšarī, 192, Ibn Yaᶜīš, X, 137).

6- The f's assimilation to the f:

An example is a reading of the sur. 2: 213 *(wa-mā ḫtala(f) ffīhi)* "Did not differ" (cf. Howell, IV, fasc. II, 1800).

7- The q's assimilation to the q:

An example is a reading of the sur. 9: 99 *(wa-yattaḫiḏu mā yunfi(q) qqurbātin)* "And look on their payments as pious gifts bringing them nearer to God" (cf. Ibn Ya^cīš, X, 138); and the sur. 7: 143 *(fa-lammā ᵓafā(q) qqāla)* "When he recovered his senses he said" (cf. Zamaḫšarī, 193, Ibn Yaᶜīš, X, 138).

8- The k's assimilation to the k:

An example is a reading of the sur. 20: 35 *(ᶜinna(k) kkunta)* "For Thou art He" (cf. Ibn Yaᶜīš, X, 138); and sur. 20: 33 *(kay nusabbiḥa(k) kkaṯīran wa-naḏkura(k) kkaṯṯīran)* "That we may celebrate Thy praise without stint, and remember Thee withou stint" (cf. Zamaḫšarī, 193, Ibn Yaᶜīš, X, 138).

9- The m's assimilation to the m:

An example is a reading of the sur. 1: 2-3 *(ᵓal-raḥī(m) mmāliki yawmi l-dīni)* "Most Merciful; Master of the Day of Judgment" (cf. Ibn Yaᶜīš, X, 147).

10- The h's assimilation to the h:

An example is a reading of the sur. 25: 43 *(ᵓilāha(h) hhawāᵓu)* "[As taketh] for his god his own passion (or impulse)?", read so by Abū ᶜAmr (cf. Ibn ᶜUṣfūr, II, 726).

11- The y's assimilation to the y:

An example is a reading of the sur. 11: 66 *(wa-min ḫiz(y) yyawmaʾiḏin)* "And from the Ignominy of that Day", read so by Abū ᶜAmr (cf. Ibn ᶜUṣfūr, II, 725).

12- The w's assimilation to the w:

An example is *(ʾiḫša(w) wwāqidan* (cf. Sībawaihi, II, 457) "Fear [2nd person of the masc. pl. of the imperative] one who sets fire!".

1.3.3. The sequence of two identical segments of which the 1st is vowelled and the 2nd vowelless: the prohibition of the assimilation. The assimilation in some anomalous cases. The elision of one of the identical segments. The substitution of one of the identical segments by a yāʾ:

There are four possibilities that can be considered concerning the sequence of a vowelled segment followed by a vowelless identical segment. One of them is that the assimilation is forbidden, the second one is that the assimilation is possible, the third one is that of one of the segments is elided, and the fourth one is that one of the segments is substituted by a *y*. Furthermore, it can be noted that the sequence of a vowelled segment preceding a vowelless segment can only occur in one word, and not in two words following each other on account that the 1st segment in the second word can only be vowelled and not vowelless, as it is impossible to begin the word with a vowelless segment in Arabic.

1- The prohibition of the assimilation:

The sequence of two identical segments of which the 1st is vowelled and the 2nd is vowelless forbids the assimilation in most of the cases because the condition of the assimilation is that the 2nd segment should be vowelled.

As examples, the forms of the doubled verb occurring in the perfect, imperfect and imperative in which the vowelled agent pronouns are suffixed to, can be taken up. The 3rd radical is vowelless in them to prevent the disliked succession of four vowelled segments. Hence the sequence is that of a vowelled segment preceding a vowelless segment.

In the case of the perfect, the vowelled agent pronouns are the *-tu* "/1st person of the sing.", the *-ta* "2nd person of the masc. sing.", the *-ti* "2nd person of the fem sing., the *-n(a)ā* "1st person of the pl.", the *-tum* "2nd person of the masc. pl.", the *-tunna* "2nd person of the fem. pl." and the *-na* "3rd person of the fem. pl.". Hence the forms implied for instance by the example *madada* "to stretch" are: *madad-tu, madad-ta, madad-ti, madad-n(a)ā, madad-tum, madad-tunna* and *madad-na* which all occur with the elision of the fatḥa from the 2nd *d* of *madada.*

The vowelled agent suffix pronoun in the cases of the imperfect and of the imperative is the *-na.* It marks the 2nd and 3rd person of the fem. pl. in the case of the imperfect, namely *tamdud-na* "you stretch /fem. pl." and *yamdud-na* "they stretch /fem. pl." respectively, and the 2nd person of the fem. pl. in the case of the imperative, namely *ʾumdud-na* "stretch!". In all these cases the assimilation of the two identical segments, namely the 2nd radical vowelled *d,* the *du,* to the 3rd radical vowelless *d* is forbidden because of the vowellessness of this 2nd *d* that has lost its vowel in order to prevent the succession of the vowels when the suffixed *-na* of the fem. pl. is suffixed to the word, and because this vowellessness marks as well the imperative.

2- The assimilation in some anomalous cases:

The assimilation of the two identical segments of which the 1st is vowelled and the 2nd vowelless is carried out in some anomalous cases, as in some cases of doubled verbs occurring in the imperative in which the assimilation of the identical segments is carried out in spite of the vowelless state of the 2nd segment following a vowelless segment, which by principle should prevent the assimilation.

An example is the imperative of the 2nd person of the masc. sing. *ᵓumdud* "stretch!" with the 1st *d* vowelled by a ḍamma and the 2nd *d* vowelless, which becomes *mudda, muddi* and *muddu* (cf. Åkesson, *Ibn Masᶜūd* 196: fol. 18b, Wright, II, 70). Those who dissolute are the Ḥiǧāzīs whereas those who assimilate are the people of Tamīm (cf. Wright, II, 70 in the notes).

By contrast to the variant of the imperative of the 2nd person of the masc. sing. *muddu* in which the ḍamma is given to the *d* on the analogy of the ḍamma of the 1st radical *m,* it is impossible to use the variant *firru* "flee!" for the imperative of the 2nd person of the masc. sing. of *farra* "to flee", with the ḍamma vowelling the *r* instead of the usual form *ᵓifrir,* as the ḍamma is disliked after the kasra of the 1st radical (cf. ibid). However *firra* and *firri* are possible variants to be used instead of *ᵓifrir,* with the fatḥa and the kasra vowelling the r respectively (cf. de Sacy, I, 229, Wright, II, 70), as *mudda* and *muddi* mentioned above.

As well in other examples, both *ᶜaḍḍa* and *ᶜaḍḍi* are used as well as variants with the assimilation of the ḍāds instead of *ᵓiᶜḍaḍ* bite! /masc. sing. (cf. Wright, II, 70)

3- The elision of one of the identical segments:

The elision of one of the identical segments is a possibility in some anomalous cases.

An example is the perfect of the 2nd person of the masc. sing. *ẓalil-ta* "you continued all day" and of the 2nd person of the fem. sing. *ẓalil-ti* that becomes after the elision of one of the lāms *ẓal-ta* and *ẓal-ti* respectively (cf. Ibn Mālik, *La Alfīya* 222, Ibn ᶜAqīl, II, 584, Åkesson, *Ibn Masᶜūd* 196: fol. 18b, Wright, II, 69, Howell, IV, fasc. II, 1836 sqq., de Sacy, I, 228). The alleviated form *ẓalta* occurs in the sur. 20: 97 *(l-laḏī ẓalta ᶜalayhi ᶜākifan)* "Of whom thou hast become a devoted worshipper", and *ẓaltum* in the sur. 56: 65 *(fa-ẓaltum tafakkahūna)* "And ye would be left in wonderment" (cf. Howell, IV, fasc. II, 1836).

It can be remarked that in the dialectal variant of the Banū ᶜĀmir, the 2nd radical *l* of the perfect of the 1st person of the sing. *ẓaliltu* is elided, and the fatḥa which is the vowelling of the 1st radical remains unchanged, namely *ẓaltu,* whereas in the dialect of the Ḥiǧāzīs the 2nd radical is elided after that its kasra is shifted to the 1st radical, namely *ẓiltu* (cf. ᶜAbd al-Ḥamīd, *Taṣrīf* 611, Talmon, *ᶜAyn* 184).

Concerning the variant *ẓiltu,* Sībawaihi, II, 446 notes that they compared it to *lastu* "I am not". Both *ẓiltu* and *ẓaltu* can occur in this verse said by ᶜUmar b. Abī Rabīᶜa al-Maḫzūmi, cited by ᶜAbd al-Ḥamīd, *Taṣrīf* 611 in the note:

> *"Ẓiltu fīhā ḏāta yawma wāqifan*
> *ᵓasᵓalu l-manzila hal fīhi ḫabar".*
> "And this day I remained standing by it,
> asking the house if it had any news".

Both *ẓiltu* or *ẓaltu* with the elision of the l and maliltu with its maintainance are combined in this verse said by ᶜUmar b. Abī Rabīᶜa, cited by ᶜAbd al-Ḥamīd, *Taṣrīf* 611 in the note:

> *"wa-mā maliltu wa-lākin zāda ḥubbukum*
> *wa-mā ḏakartuki ᵓillā ẓiltu (/ẓaltu] ka-l-sadiri".*
> "I did not become weary but my love for you has increased.
> Whenever I think of you I become as the possessed".

Another example is the imperative of the 2nd person of the pl. *ᵓiqrir-na* "stay quietly!" that becomes after the elision of one of the rāᵓs *qir-na. ᵓiqrir-na* is from the root *q r r* with 2nd and 3rd radical r (cf. Ibn Manẓūr, V, 3578-3579), in which the 2nd *r* is vowelless on the basis that the sukūn marks the imperative and that the vowelled agent pronoun is suffixed to it. The sequence of the identical segments in *ᵓiqrir-na* is that of a vowelled segment, namely the 2nd radical *r,* preceding a vowelless segment, namely the 3rd radical *r,* which by principle should prevent the assimilation. The elision of the 1st *r* of the sequence is however a possibility after that its vowel is shifted to the *q,* and then the hamza of the imperative is also elided as it is not more needed now that the 1st radical *q* is vowelled. The resulting alleviated form is *qir-na* (cf. Ibn ᶜAqīl, II, 584-585, Åkesson, *Ibn Masᶜūd* 196: fol. 18b, Penrice, *Dictionary* 116). The variant *qarna* exists as well which pertains to another dialectal variant, and its base form is then the variant *ᵓiqrar-na.* It can be mentioned that *wa-qarna* occurs instead of *wa-qirna* in the sur. 33: 33 *(wa-qarna fī buyūtikunna)* and that it is the reading of Nāfi[c] and [c]Āṣim (cf. Ibn [c]Aqīl, II, 585).

4- The substitution of one of the identical segments by a y:

The substitution of one of the identical segments by a *y* is another alternative in some anomalous cases. Sībawaihi, II, 447 mentions the following verbs of Form V in which this substitution has been carried out (cf. Roman, *Étude I,* 361):

- Form V *tasarrartu* "I had a concubine" that becomes after the change of the 3rd radical *r* into a *y tasarraytu.*

- Form V *taẓannantu* "I formed an opinion" that becomes after the change of the 3rd radical *n* into a *y taẓannaytu.*

- Form V *taqaṣṣaṣtu* "I remembered [his words]" that becomes after the change of 3rd radical *ṣ* into a *y taqaṣṣaytu.*

- Form V *taqaḍḍiya* used instead of *taqaḍḍaḍa* "to fly down swiftly" (cf. Zamaḫšarī, 173, Åkesson, *Ibn Mas[c]ūd* 194: fol. 17b), in which the 3rd radical *ḍ* is changed into the *y,* and the *ḍ* is vowelled with a kasra instead of a fatḥa. The verb is found in the example *taqaḍḍiya l-bāzī* "the hawk flew down swiftly" of the verse said by [c]Aǧǧāǧ cited by Ibn Ǧinnī, *Sirr II,* 759, Mu[ɔ]addib, *Taṣrīf* 438, Ibn Ya[c]īš, X, 24, Åkesson, *Ibn Mas[c]ūd* 204: (170):

"ʾIḏā l-kirāmu btadarū l-bāʿa badar
taqaḍḍiya l-bāzī ʾiḏā l-bāzī kasar".
"When the generous hasten to the noble deed,
he hastens with the swoop of the falcon, when the
falcon contracts his wings".

The substistution of the *y* for the 3rd radical occurs in other forms than Form V. The following cases can be mentioned:

- Form IV *ʾamlaltu* "I dictated" that becomes after the change of 3rd radical l into a *y* *ʾamlaytu* (cf. Sībawaihi, II, 447, Roman, Étude I, 361).

- Form VIII *yaʾtammu* in which the 2nd *m* is substituted by the yāʾ and becomes *yaʾtamī* "he takes example". It occurs in this verse said by Kuṯayyir, *Dīwān* 300 in which he is praising ʿAbd al-ʿAzīz b. Marwān. It is cited by Ibn Ğinni, *Sirr II,* 760, Zamaḫšarī, 173, Ibn Yaʿīš, X, 24, *Mulūkī* 252, Ibn ʿUṣfūr, I, 374, Howell, IV, fasc. I, 1292:

"Nazūru mraʾan ʾammā l-ʾilāha fa-yattaqī
wa-ʾammā bi-fiʿli l-ṣāliḥīna fa-yaʾtamī".
"We will visit a man such that, whatever betide,
God he fears,
and, whatever betide, by the deed of the righteous
he takes example".

This change of the 2nd segment among the doubled segments into a *y* is carried out as well in nominal forms, e.g. the *maṣdar*

Form II *taṣdiyat* for *taṣdidat* that occurs in the sur. 8: 35 *(wa-mā kāna ṣalātuhum ᶜinda l-bayti ᵓillā mukāᵓan wa-taṣdiyatan)* "Their prayers at the House (of God) is nothing but whistling and clapping of hands".

1.4. The sequence of two different segments: cases in which the assimilation is or is not carried out

The sequence of two different segments can result in the assimilation of one to the other on the condition that they originate from the same point of articulation or from two close points of articulation. The following sequences in which the vowelling or the absence of a vowel of one of the segments are taken up:

1.4.1. the sequence of two different segments of which the 1st is vowelless and the 2nd is vowelled: the assimilation.

1.4.2. the sequence of two different segments which are both vowelled: the assimilation.

1.4.1. The sequence of two different segments of which the 1st is vowelless and the 2nd is vowelled: the assimilation:

The vowelless state of the 1st segment preceding a vowelled segment that is close to it in the point of articulation or that is akin to it in character or that is different and having a stronger character than it, can result in the assimilation.

This sequence can be found in one word or in two words following each other, the latter pertaining to the rarities.

1.4.1.1. The assimilation that is carried out from the 1st vowelless segment to a 2nd different vowelled segment in one word:

The following assimilations can be mentioned:

1- the assimilation of the vowelless *l*- of the definite article *al*- to the vowelled solar segment of the word that it is prefixed to.

2- the assimilation of the 3rd radical *d* of a verb in the perfect to the pronoun of the agent beginning with the *t* that is suffixed to it, and 3)- the vowelled infixed *t* of Form VIII *ʾiftaʿala* to the 1st vowelless radical preceding it.

1- The assimilation of the vowelless l- of the article al- to the vowelled solar segment that begins a noun:

This assimilation is carried out in some examples of definite nouns to which the article *al*- is prefixed to, which begin with one of the "solar segments", namely the *t, ṯ, d, ḏ, r, z, s, š, ṣ, ḍ, ṭ, ẓ, l* and *n* (cf. Wright, I, 15, Bakkūš, *Taṣrīf* 66). In these examples, the vowelless *l-* is assimilated to the vowelled solar segment following it. An example is الرَّحْمٰن *al-Raḥmān* "the Merciful" in which the *r* carries the *šadda* in Arabic as an indication of the assimilation of the *l-* to it (cf. par. 1.1.). The reason why the *l-* is assimilated to those segments is that they all originate from between the teeth to the lower part of the palate, and thus are all close to the point of articulation of the *l* (cf. Bakkūš, *Taṣrīf* 66).

2- The assimilation of the 3rd radical d in verbs that occur in the perfect, to the vowelled suffixed pronoun of the agent that begins with the t:

In the cases of verbs whose 3rd radical is a *d* that occur in the perfect in the persons in which the vowelled pronoun of the agent beginning with the *t* is suffixed to, namely the *-tu* "1st person of the sing.", *-ta* "2nd person of the masc. sing.", *-ti* "2nd person of the fem. sing.", *-tum* "2nd person of the masc. pl.", *-tunna* "2nd person of the fem. pl." and *-tumā* "2nd person of the dual", an assimilation is carried out from the vowelless *d* to the vowelled *t* following it (cf. Vernier, I, 57).

Some examples are *madad-tu* "I stretched", *madad-ta* "you stretched /masc. sing." and *madad-ti* "you stretched /fem. sing.", in which the *d* is assimilated to the *t* which is indicated in Arabic by the *šadda* over the *t*. The reason of this assimilation is the proximity of the *d* to the *t* in the point of articulation as they both are alveolars (for the segments see par. 1.2.1.).

3- The assimilation that is carried out between the vowelled infixed t of Form VIII of the perfect ʾiftaʿala and the 1st vowelless radical preceding it:

The infixed *t* of Form VIII of the perfect *ʾiftaʿala* is either assimilated to or is assimilated by one of the vowelless fourteen segments preceding it that is the 1st radical (for a general study of this assimilation see Wright, II, 66-67, Howell, IV, fasc. II, 1803 sqq.). These segments are: 1- the ʾ, 2- *t*, 3- *ṯ*, 4- *d*, 5- *ḏ*, 6- *z*, 7- *s*, 8- *š*, 9- *ṣ*, 10- *ḍ*, 11- *ṭ*, 12- *ẓ*, 13- *w* and 14- *y* (cf. Åkesson, *Ibn Masʿūd* 196-198: fol. 19a).

It is possible to distinguish between cases in which the 1st vowelless radical is assimilated to the infixed vowelled *t* of Form VIII of the perfect *ʾiftaʿala* (cf. 1.4.1.1.3.1.) and cases in which the infixed vowelled *t* of Form VIII of the perfect *ʾiftaʿala* is assimilated to the 1st vowelless radical (cf. 1.4.1.1.3.2.).

1.4.1.1.3.1. Cases in which the 1st vowelless radical is assimilated to the infixed vowelled t of Form VIII of the perfect ʾiftaʿala:

The 1st vowelless radical is assimilated to the vowelled infixed *t* if it is a: 1- ʾ, 2- *t*, 3- possibly *ṯ*, 4- *w* and 5- *y*.

The phonological procedure that is carried out in the perfect of Form VIII can be illustrated as follows: *ʾiftaʿala* with the vowelless 1st radical *f* followed by the vowelled infix *t* becomes *ʾittaʿala* after that the 1st radical *f* is assimilated to the vowelled *t.*

1- The assimilation of the 1st radical vowelless ʾ to the vowelled infixed t of Form VIII ʾiftaʿala:

An example is Form VIII *ʾiʾtaḫaḏa* which becomes after the assimilation *ʾittaḫaḏa* "to take" (cf. Åkesson, *Ibn Masʿūd* 196: fol. 19a, Howell, IV, fasc. II, 1848 sqq., de Sacy, I, 236, Wright, II, 76-77, Lane, I, 29, Fleisch, *Traité I,* 150). The base form *ʾiʾtaḫaḏa* is from *ʾaḫaḏa* "to take", a verb with 1st hamza radical. The process leading to the assimilation is not a direct process and involves as well the substitutions of segments, namely the *y* for the *ʾ* and the *t* for the *y*. For this reason this assimilation is considered as anomalous. The changes can be illustrated with the following: *ʾiʾtaḫaḏa* with the vowelless *ʾ* preceded by a kasra becomes *ʾiytaḫaḏa* with the *ʾ* changed into a *y* on account of the influence of the kasra preceding it. As the vowelless *y* precedes the vowelled *t,* the *y* is changed into the *t* and then the *t* is assimilated to the *t* so that it becomes *ʾittaḫaḏa* (إِتَّخَذَ). This change of the *y,* which is not the underlying radical from the form *ʾiytaḫaḏa,* into the *t* resulting in *ʾittaḫaḏa,* is considered as anomalous because the *y* is already substituted for the *ʾ* that is the radical of the form *ʾiʾtaḫaḏa.* For this reason some grammarians preferred to believe that *ʾittaḫaḏa* is formed from the variant *taḫiḏa* and not from *ʾaḫaḏa,* and their theory was integrated in the language (cf. Ibn Manẓūr, I, 37, Zaǧǧāǧī, *Maǧālis* 333, Wright, II, 76-77, Lane, I, 29, Fleisch, *Traité I,* 150).

2- The assimilation of the 1st radical vowelless t to the vowelled infixed t of Form VIII ʾiftaᶜala:

An example is Form VIII *ʾittaǧara* "to trade" that becomes after the assimilation *ʾittaǧara* with one *t* carrying the šadda in Arabic as an indication of the assimilation (cf. par. 1.3.1.1.).

3- The assimilation between the 1st radical vowelless t and the vowelled infixed t of Form VIII ʾiftaᶜala:

The vowelless 1st radical *ṯ* can be assimilated to the vowelled infixed *t* as well as the vowelled infixed *t* can be assimilated to the vowelless 1st radical *ṯ*. An example is Form VIII *ʾiṯtaʾara* "to get one's revenge" (cf. Åkesson, *Ibn Masᶜūd* 196: fol. 19a) with the vowelless *ṯ* preceding the vowelled *t* that can become after the assimilation of the *t* to the *ṯ* *ʾiṯṯaʾara* or after the assimilation of the *ṯ* to the *t* *ʾittaʾara.*

4- The assimilation of the 1st radical vowelless w to the vowelled infixed t of Form VIII ʾiftaᶜala:

An example is Form VIII *ʾiwtaᶜada* "to accept a promise" (from *waᶜada* "to promise") with the vowelless *w* preceding the vowelled *t* that becomes after the assimilation of the *w* to the *t*

ʾittaᶜada (cf. de Sacy, I, 240, Wright, II, 80-81, Lane, II, 2902, Åkesson, *Ibn Masᶜūd* 200: fol. 20a-20b).

The *w* is changed into a *y* on account of the kasra preceding it before that the assimilation to the infixed *t* is carried out. Hence *ʾiwtaᶜada* becomes at first *ʾiytaᶜada* "(cf. Wright, II, 80), and then *ʾittaᶜada.*

5- The assimilation of the 1st radical vowelless y to the vowelled infixed t of Form VIII ʾiftaᶜala:

An example is Form VIII *ʾiytasara* "to play at hazard" (cf. Zamaḫšarī, 175, 178, Åkesson, *Ibn Masᶜūd* 200: fol. 20b, de Sacy, I 240, Wright, II, 80-81) from *yasara* "to be easy", with the vowelless *y* preceding the vowelled *t,* that becomes after the assimilation *ʾittasara* with the *y* assimilated to the *t* resulting in the doubled *t.* The variant *ʾittasara* with this assimilation is preferred to the base form *ʾiytasara* because the vowelling of the *ʾ* with a kasra preceding the *y* in *ʾiytasara* is deemed as a heavy combination.

1.4.1.1.3.2. Cases in which the infixed vowelled t of Form VIII of the perfect ʾiftaᶜala is assimilated to the 1st vowelless radical preceding it:

The surd and soft infixed *t* is assimilated to the 1st radical if this radical originates from the same point of articulation or from a close point of articulation to it, and that it is stronger than it in character. Thus the surd *t* is assimilated to the 1st radical if it is a voiced segment (for the voiced and surd segments see par. 1.2.2.) because the voiced segment is considered as stronger than the surd segment in the sound (cf. Bakkūš, *Taṣrīf* 40, 66), or if it is a covered segment (cf. ibid, 66; and for the covered segments see par. 1.2.2.) or if it is a sibilant segment (for the sibilant segments see 1.2.2.) on account of the strength of character of the covered segment and of the sibilant segment in relation to the soft segment. Among the fourteen segments mentioned above (see 1.4.1.1.3.), the 1st radical's segment to which the alveolar surd and soft *t* is assimilated to can be: 1- the alveolar and voiced *d,* 2- the interdental and voiced *ḏ,* 3- the dental, voiced and sibilant *z,* 4- the dental, surd and sibilant *ṣ,* 5- the alveolar and voiced *ḍ,* 6- the alveolar and voiced *ṭ,* 7- the interdental and surd *ṯ,* 8- the dental, surd and sibilant *s* and 9- the pre-palatal and surd *š.*

The phonological procedure that is carried out in the perfect of Form VIII is illustrated as follows: *ᵓiftaᶜala* with the vowelless 1st radical *f* followed by the vowelled infix *t* becomes *ᵓiffaᶜala* after that the vowelled *t* is assimilated to the 1st radical *f.*

1- The assimilation of the vowelled infixed t of Form VIII ᵓiftaᶜala to the 1st radical vowelless d preceding it:

An example is Form VIII *ᵓidt(a)āna* "to buy upon credit" (cf. Zamaḫšarī, 176, Ibn ᶜAqīl, II, 582, Åkesson, *Ibn Masᶜūd*

198: fol. 19a, Lane, I, 942-943) with the vowelless *d* preceding the vowelled *t* that becomes after the assimilation *ʾidd(a)āna* with the *t* assimilated to the *d* resulting in the doubled *d*.

The reason of the substitution of the *d* for the *t* before that the assimilation is carried out in it resulting in the doubled *d*, is the common point of articulation of both these segments as they both are alveolars (for the segments see par. 1.2.1.). As for the reason why it is specifically the *t* that is assimilated to the *d* and not vice versa, it is so that the character of the voiced dental segment is considered as stronger than the surd segment.

ʾidt(a)āna	→	*ʾidd(a)āna*
d + *t*	→	*dd*
voiced + surd	→	voiced + voiced

2- The assimilation of the vowelled infixed t of Form VIII ʾiftaʿala to the 1st radical vowelless d preceding it:

An example is Form VIII *ʾiḏtakara* "to remember" with the vowelless *ḏ* preceding the vowelled *t* that becomes after the assimilation *ʾiḏḏakara* with the *t* assimilated to the *ḏ* resulting in the doubled *ḏ*. The reason why the *t* is assimilated to the *ḏ* and not vice versa is that the surd *t* is weaker in character than the voiced *ḏ* (cf. Bakkūš, *Taṣrīf* 66).

ʾiḏtakara	→	*ʾiḏḏakara*
ḏ + *t*	→	*ḏḏ*
voiced + surd	→	voiced + voiced

Other variants are *ʾiḏdakara* with the doubling of the *d* and *ʾiddakara* with the *d* following the *ḏ* (cf. Zamaḫšarī, 195, Ibn ᶜAqīl, II, 582, Åkesson, *Ibn Masᶜūd* 198: fol. 19a, de Sacy, I, 222, Vernier, I, 344-345, Wright, II, 66, ᶜAbd al-Tawwāb, *Taṭawwur* 29).

The process concerning the 1st variant *ʾiḏdakara* is that the *t* of the base form *ʾiḏtakara* is changed into the *d*. The reason of this substitution is the closeness of the points of articulation of the *d* and the *t* on account that they both are alveolars (for the segments see par. 1.2.1.). In the second variant *ʾiddakara,* the *ḏ* of *ʾiḏdakara* is changed into a *d* and both the *dāls* are than assimilated together. The reason why the substitution of the *d* for the *ḏ* is possible is the proximity of the alveolar *d* to the interdental *ḏ* and the similarity of both their characters as they are both voiced segments.

3- The assimilation of the vowelled infixed t of Form VIII ʾiftaᶜala to the 1st radical vowelless z preceding it:

An example is Form VIII *ʾizt(a)āna* "to be ornamented" (cf. Zamaḫšarī, 176, 196, Åkesson, *Ibn Masᶜūd* 198: fol. 19b, Wright, II, 66, Lane, I, 1279) with the vowelless *z* preceding the vowelled *t* that becomes after the assimilation *ʾizz(a)āna* with the *t* assimilated to the *z* resulting in the doubled *z*. The reason why the *t* is assimilated to the *z* is that there is a proximity between the alveolar *t* and the dental *z* (for the segments see par. 1.2.1.). As for why it is specifically the *t* that is assimilated to the *z* and not vice versa, it is that the surd and soft *t* is weaker in character than the voiced and sibilant *z* (for the segments' characters see par. 1.2.2.). Thus:

ʾizt(a)āna	→	*ʾizz(a)āna*
z + *t*	→	*zz*
voiced + surd	→	voiced + voiced
sibilant + soft	→	sibilant + sibilant

4- The assimilation of the vowelled infixed t of Form VIII ʾiftaᶜala to the 1st radical vowelless ṣ preceding it:

An example is Form VIII *ʾiṣtabara* "to acquire patience" (cf. Zamaḫšarī, 176, Åkesson, *Ibn Masᶜūd* 198: fol. 19b-20a, Wright, II, 67, Vernier, I, 345) with the vowelless *ṣ* preceding the vowelled *t* that becomes after the assimilation *ʾiṣṣabara* with the *t* assimilated to the *ṣ* resulting in the doubled *ṣ*. The reason why the *t* is assimilated to the *ṣ* is that there is a proximity between the alveolar *t* and the dental *ṣ* (for the segments see par. 1.2.1.). As for why it is the *t* that is assimilated to the *ṣ* and not vice versa, it is because the soft *t* is weaker in character than the sibilant *ṣ*. Thus:

ʾiṣtabara	→	*ʾiṣṣabara*
ṣ + *t*	→	*ṣṣ*
sibilant + soft	→	sibilant + sibilant

Another variant concerning this verb is the substitution of the emphatic *ṭ* for the *t* on account of the influence of the emphatic *ṣ*, namely *ʾiṣṭabara* for *ʾiṣtabara*.

5- The assimilation of the vowelled infixed t of Form VIII ʾiftaᶜala to the 1st radical vowelless ḍ preceding it:

An example is Form VIII *ʾiḍtaraba* "to acquire patience" (cf. Zamaḫšarī, 195, Åkesson, Ibn Masᶜūd 198-200: fol. 20a, de Sacy, I, 222, Wright, II, 67, Vernier, I, 345) with the vowelless *ḍ* preceding the vowelled *t* that becomes after the assimilation *ʾiḍḍaraba* "to be in a state of agitation" with the *t* asimilated to the *ḍ* resulting in the doubled *ḍ*. The reason why the *t* is assimilated to the *ḍ* is the proximity of their points of articulation as they both are alveolars (for the segments see par. 1.2.1.). As for why it is specifically the *t* that is assimilated to the *ḍ* and not vice versa, it is because the soft *t* is weaker in character than the covered *ḍ*. Thus:

ʾiḍtaraba	→	*ʾiḍḍaraba*
ḍ + t	→	*ḍḍ*
covered + soft	→	covered + covered

Another possibility concerning this verb is the substitution of the *ṭ* for the *t* on account of the influence of the preceding 1st radical emphatic *ḍ*, namely *ʾiḍṭaraba* instead of *ʾiḍtaraba.*

<u>*6- The assimilation of the vowelled infixed t of Form VIII ʾiftaʿala to the 1st radical vowelless ṭ preceding it:*</u>

An example is Form VIII *ʾiṭtalaba* "to seek" (cf. Zamaḫšarī, 195, Ibn Yaʿīš, X, 46, Åkesson, *Ibn Masʿūd* 200: fol. 20a, Wright, II, 67) with the vowelless *ṭ* preceding the vowelled *t* that becomes after the assimilation *ʾiṭṭalaba* with the *t* assimilated to the *ṭ* resulting in the doubled *ṭ*. The reason why the *t* is assimilated to the *ṭ* is their common point of articulation as they are both alveolars (for the segments see par. 1.2.1.). As for why it is specifically the *t* that is assimilated to the *ṭ* and not vice versa, it is because the soft *t* is weaker in character than the covered *ṭ*. Thus:

ʾiṭtalaba	→	*ʾiṭṭalaba*
ṭ + t	→	*ṭṭ*
covered + soft	→	covered + covered

7- The assimilation of the vowelled infixed t of Form VIII ʾiftaʿala to the 1st radical vowelless ẓ preceding it:

An example is Form VIII *ʾiẓtalama* "to take upon oneself the bearing of the wrong" with the vowelless *ẓ* preceding the vowelled *t* that becomes after the assimilation *ʾiẓẓalama* (cf. Åkesson, *Ibn Masʿūd* 200: fol. 20a). The reason why the *t* is assimilated to the *ẓ* is the proximity of the point of articulation of the alveolar *t* to the interdental *ẓ* (for the segments see par. 1.2.1). As for why it is the *t* that is specifically assimilated to the *ẓ* and not vice versa, it is that the soft *t* is weaker in character than the covered *ẓ*.

ʾiẓtalama	→	*ʾiẓẓalama*
ẓ + *t*	→	*ẓẓ*
covered + soft	→	covered + covered

Two other variants exist namely *ʾiẓṭalama* and *ʾiṭṭalama* (cf. Sībawaihi, II, 472, Ibn Ǧinnī, *Sirr I,* 224, *de Flexione* 29, Zamaḫšarī, 195, Ibn Yaʿīš, X, 47, Åkesson, *Ibn Masʿūd* 200: fol. 20a, Wright, II, 67, Lane, II, 1921, Vernier, I, 345, Howell, IV, fasc. II, 1813).

As what regards the variant *ʾiẓṭalama,* the *t* of its base form *ʾiẓtalama* is changed into the *ṭ* on account of the proximity of the points of articulation of the *t* and *ṭ,* as they both are alveolars (for the segments see 1.2.1.). As for why the *t* is assimilated to the *ṭ*, it is because the soft *t* is weaker in character than the covered *ṭ*.

Concerning the variant *ˀiṭṭalama,* the ẓāˀs from the variant *ˀiẓẓalama* are changed into the ṭāˀs. This substitution of the *ṭ* for the *ẓ* and vice versa is possibly carried out because of both these segments' common character in being among the emphatic segments. It can be mentioned that both Form I of the passive *yuẓlamu* and Form VIII of the active voice *yaẓṭalimu* occur in this verse said by Zuhair b. Abī Sulmā al-Muzanī praising Harim b. Sinān, cited by Sībawaihi, II, 472, Ibn Ǧinnī, *Sirr I,* 219, Muˀaddib, *Taṣrīf* 170 Zamaḫšarī, 195, Ibn Yaᶜīš, X, 47, Howell, IV, fasc. II, 1813, Åkesson, *Ibn Masᶜūd* 229: (197):

> *"Huwa l-ǧawādu l-laḏī yuᶜṭīka nāᶜilahu*
> *ᶜafwan wa-yuẓlamu ˀaḥyānan fa-yaẓṭalimu".*
> "He is the magnanimous, who gives you his
> largesse spontaneously; and is wronged at times,
> and than puts up with that wrong".

All the three variants *fa-yaẓẓalimu, fa-yaṭṭalimu* or *fa-yaẓṭalimu* as being the last word of the rime have been cited in different works (cf. Fischer/Braūnlich, *Šawāhid* 227).

8- The assimilation of the vowelled infixed t of Form VIII ˀiftaᶜala to the 1st radical vowelless t preceding it:

An example is Form VIII *ˀiṯtaˀara* "to get one's revenge" that becomes after the assimilation *ˀiṯṯaˀara* (cf. 1.4.1.1.3.1.:3).

9- The assimilation of the vowelled infixed t of Form VIII ʾiftaʿala to the 1st radical vowelless s preceding it:

An example is Form VIII *ʾistamaʿa* "to listen" with the vowelless *s* preceding the vowelled *t* that becomes after the assimilation of the *t* to the *s ʾissamaʿa* (cf. Sībawaihi, II, 472, Zamaḫšarī, 196, Åkesson, *Ibn Masʿūd* 198: fol. 19b, de Sacy, I, 220, Wright, II, 66).

The reason why it is possible to substitute the *s* for the *t* is that they originate from close points of articulation, as the alveolar *t* is close to the dental *s* (for the segments see par. 1.2.1.) and they are both similar in character in being among the surd segments (for the segments' characters see par. 1.2.2.). However it is only the *t* than can be assimilated to the *s* and not vice versa because the *s* is a sibilant segment, and thus offers a stronger character than the *t*.

ʾistamaʿa	→	*ʾissamaʿa*
s + t	→	*ss*
sibilant + soft	→	sibilant + sibilant

It can be noted that the variant *yassamiʿu* with the assimilation has been anomalously read by some instead of *yastamiʿu* in the sur. 6: 25 i.e. *(wa-minhum man yassamiʿu ʾilayka)* "Of them there are some who (pretend to) listen to thee". Furthermore the variant *yassamaʿūna* of the sur. 37: 8 *(lā yassammaʿūna ʾilā l-malāʾi l-ʾaʿlā)* "(So) they should not strain their ears in the direction of the Exalted Assembly" is Form V *yatasamma^{c}ūna* originally and not Form VIII *yastami^{c}ūna* in which the *t* is assimilated to the *s*. Some read the sur. with Form I *yasma^{c}ūna* instead for the sake of alleviation (cf. Ibn Manẓūr, III, 2095).

10- The assimilation of the vowelled infixed t of Form VIII ʾifta^{c}ala to the 1st radical vowelless š preceding it:

An example is Form VIII *ʾištabaha* "to liken" with the vowelless *š* preceding the vowelled *t* that becomes *ʾiššabaha* after the assimilation of the *t* to the *š* (cf. Åkesson, *Ibn Mas^{c}ūd* 198: fol. 19b).

The reason why this substitution is possible is the proximity of the point of articulation of the alveolar *t* to the pre-palatal *š* (for the segments see par. 1.2.1.) and both these segments' common character in being among the surd segments (for the segments' characters see par. 1.2.2.).

1.4.1.2. The assimilation that is carried out from the 1st vowelless segment to a 2nd different vowelled segment in two words following each other:

The assimilation can be carried out from a 1st vowelless segment which is the last segment of a word to a 2nd vowelled segment that is the initial segment of the word following it (for some references to different works that treat this sort of assimilation see 1.3.), if both different segments originate from a common point of articulation of from close points of articulation.

An example is the reading of the sur. 4: 81 *bayyat ṭāʾifatun* in which the surd and soft *t* is assimilated to the voiced and covered *ṭ* resulting in *bayyat ṭṭāʾifatun* (بَيَّت طّائفة) "A section of them meditate all night" (cf. Cantineau, *Études* 35). The sentence is written in Arabic with the *t,* which is the last segment of the first word *bayyat* without any vowel or sukūn, and with the *ṭ* which is the initial segment of the second word given a *šadda* as an indication of the assimilation. As what regards the common point of articulation of the *t* and the *ṭ* that enables the substitution of the *ṭ* for the *t* leading to the assimilation, they are both alveolars (for the segments see 1.2.1.). As for their characters, the covered *ṭ* is stronger than the soft *t,* which explains why it is the *t* specifically that is assimilated to the *ṭ* and not vice versa.

1.4.2. The sequence of two different segments which are both vowelled: the assimilation:

The vowelled state of the 1st segment preceding another different vowelled one that originates from the same point of articulation as it, or from a close point of articulation to it, or that is akin to it in character, can result in the assimilation. This sequence can be found as well in one word or in two words following each other, the latter pertaining to the rarities.

1.4.2.1. The assimilation that is carried out from the 1st vowelled segment to a 2nd vowelled segment in one word:

The cases that are here discussed are the assimilation of the vowelled prefixed *t* of Form V *tafa*ᶜᶜ*ala* or Form VI *taf(a)ā*ᶜ*ala* to the 1st vowelled radical following it (cf. par. 1.4.2.1.1.) and of the vowelled infixed *t* of Form VIII of the imperfect *yafta*ᶜ*ilu* to the 2nd vowelled radical following it (cf. par. 1.4.2.1.2.).

*1.4.2.1.1. The assimilation of the vowelled prefixed t of Form V tafa*ᶜᶜ*ala or Form VI taf(a)ā*ᶜ*ala to the 1st vowelled radical following it:*

The prefixed *t* of Form V and VI is assimilated to the 1st radical of the verb (cf. Zamaḫšarī, 196, Åkesson, *Ibn Mas*ᶜ*ūd* 202: fol. 21a, de Sacy, I, 220-221, Wright, II, 64-65, ᶜAbd al-Tawwāb, *Taṭawwur* 29) following it if it is: 1- the *t* (for the assimilation of two identical segments see par. 1.3.2.1.), 2- the interdental and surd *ṯ*, 3- the alveolar and voiced *d*, 4- the interdental and voiced *ḏ*, 5- the dental, voiced and sibilant *z*, 6- the dental, surd and sibilant *s*, 7- the pre-palatal and surd *š*, 8- the dental, surd and sibilant *ṣ*, 9- the alveolar and voiced *ḍ*, 10- the alveolar and voiced *ṭ*, or 11- the interdental and voiced *ẓ*.

The assimilation implies that the prefixed *t* loses its vowel and that the prosthetic hamza vowelled by a kasra, the *ʾi,* is prefixed to the word to avoid beginning it with a vowelless segment.

The phonological procedure that is carried out in the perfect of Form V can be illustrated as follows: *tafaᶜᶜala* with the vowelled *t* prefix preceding the vowelled 1st radical *f* becomes *ffaᶜᶜala* after that the *t's* fatḥa is elided and the *t* is assimilated to the 1st radical *f* vowelled by a fatḥa. As it is prohibited to begin the word with a vowelless 1st radical *f,* the *ʾi* is prefixed so that it becomes *ʾiffaᶜᶜala.*

The same procedure is carried as what concerns Form VI *taf(a)āᶜala* that becomes *ʾiff(a)āᶜala.*

It can be remarked that the prosthetic alif is not needed in the imperfect of Form V *ʾiffaᶜᶜala* that becomes *yaffaᶜᶜalu* and Form VI *ʾiff(a)āᶜala* that becomes *yaff(a)āᶜalu.*

1- The assimilation of the vowelled prefixed t of Form V tafaᶜᶜala or Form VI taf(a)āᶜala to the 1st vowelled radical t following it:

This assimilation has been taken up within the sub-paragraph discussing the assimilation of two vowelled identical segments (cf. 1.3.2.1.). The example there is Form V *tatarrasa* "shielded himself" that becomes after the assimilation *ʾittarasa.*

2- The assimilation of the vowelled prefixed t of Form V tafa^{cc}ala or Form VI taf(a)ā^{c}ala to the 1st vowelled radical ṯ following it:

An example is Form VI *taṯ(a)āqala* "to be borne down heavily" that becomes after the assimilation *ʾiṯṯ(a)āqala* (cf. Åkesson, *Ibn Mas^{c}ūd* 202: fol. 21a, Howell, IV, fasc. II, 1829, Lane, I, 344, Penrice, *Dictionary* 25). The vowelled alveolar and surd *t* prefix vowelled by a fatḥa, the *ta,* is assimilated to the vowelled interdental and surd 1st radical *ṯ* vowelled by a fatḥa, the *ṯa,* resulting in *ṯṯāqala* and the prosthetic hamza vowelled by a kasra, the *ʾi,* is prefixed to prevent beginning the word with a vowelless segment. I can mention that the 2nd person of the masc. pl. *ʾiṯṯāqaltum* occurs in the sur. 9: 38 *(ʾiṯṯāqaltum ʾilā l-ʾarḍi fī sabīli l-lāhi)* "In the Cause of God ye cling heavily to the earth?".

3- The assimilation of the vowelled prefixed t of Form V tafa^{cc}ala or Form VI taf(a)ā^{c}ala to the 1st vowelled radical d following it:

An example is Form VI *tad(a)āraʾa* "to repel" that becomes after the assimilation *ʾidd(a)āraʾa* (cf. Howell, IV, fasc. II, 1829, Lane, I, 865, Penrice, *Dictionary* 47). The vowelled alveolar and surd *t* prefix vowelled by a fatḥa, the *ta,* is assimilated to the vowelled alveolar and voiced 1st radical *d* vowelled by a fatḥa, the *da,* resulting in *ʾidd(a)āraʾa* and the prosthetic hamza vowelled by a kasra, the *ʾi,* is prefixed to prevent beginning the word with a vowelless segment. I can mention that the 2nd person of the masc. pl. *fa-ddāraʾtum* occurs in the sur. 2: 72 *(fa-ddāraʾtum fīhā)* "And fell into a dispute among yourselves as to the crime:".

4- The assimilation of the vowelled prefixed t of Form V tafaᶜᶜala or Form V taf(a)āᶜala to the 1st vowelled radical ḏ following it:

An example is Form VI *taḏ(a)ākara* "to be reminded" that becomes after the assimilation *ʾiḏḏ(a)ākara* (cf. Howell, IV, fasc. II, 1829, Lane, I, 968, Penrice, *Dictionary* 52). The vowelled alveolar and surd *t* prefix, the *ta,* is assimilated to the vowelled interdental and voiced 1st radical *ḏa* resulting in *ḏḏ(a)ākara* and the prosthetic hamza vowelled by a kasra, the *ʾi,* is prefixed to prevent beginning the word with a vowelless segment. Form V of the imperfect of the 3rd person of the masc. sing. *yaḏḏakkaru* occurs in both the sur. 80: 3-4 *(wa-mā yudrīka laᶜallahu yazzakkā ʾaw yaḏḏakkaru fa-tanfaᶜahu l-ḏikrā)* "But what could tell thee but that perchance he might grow (in spiritual understanding)? Or that he might receive admonition, and he teaching might profit him?", and the sur. 2: 269 *(wa-mā yaḏḏakkaru ʾillā ʾūlū l-ʾalbābi)* "But none will grasp the Message but men of understanding".

5- The assimilation of the vowelled prefixed t of Form V tafa^{cc}ala or Form VI taf(a)ā^{c}ala to the 1st vowelled radical z following it:

An example is Form V *tazayyana* "to decorate itself" that becomes after the assimilation *ʾizzayyana* (cf. Howell, IV, fasc. II, 1829, Lane, I, 1279, Wright, II, 64, Penrice, *Dictionary* 64). The alveolar and soft vowelled *t* prefix, the *ta,* is assimilated to the vowelled dental and sibilant 1st radical *z,* the *za,* resulting in *zzayyana* and the prosthetic hamza vowelled by a kasra, the *ʾi,* is prefixed to prevent beginning the word with a vowelless segment. It can be mentioned that the 3rd person of the fem. sing. *wa-zzayyanat* occurs in the sur. 10: 24 *(ḥattā ʾiḏā ʾaḫaḏati l-ʾarḍu zuḫrufahā wa-zzayyanat)* "Till the earth is clad with its golden ornaments and is decked out (in beauty)".

6- The assimilation of the vowelled prefixed t of Form V tafa^{cc}ala or Form VI taf(a)ā^{c}ala to the 1st vowelled radical s following it:

An example is Form V *tasamma^{c}a* "to listen" that becomes after the assimilation *ʾissamma^{c}a* originally (cf. Howell, IV, fasc. II, 1829, Lane, I, 1427, 1428, Wright, II, 65, Penrice, *Dictionary* 72). The vowelled alveolar and soft *t* prefix, the *ta,* is assimilated to the vowelled dental and sibilant 1st radical *s,* the *sa,* resulting in *ssamma^{c}a* and the prosthetic hamza vowelled by a kasra, the *ʾi,* is prefixed to prevent beginning the word with a vowelless segment. It can be mentioned that the imperfect of the 3rd person of the masc. pl. *yassammaᶜūna* occurs in the sur. 37: 8 *(lā yassammaᶜūna ᵓilā l-malāᵓi l-ᵓaᶜlā)* "(So) they should not strain their ears in the direction of the Exalted Assembly".

7- The assimilation of the vowelled prefixed t of Form V tafaᶜᶜala or Form VI taf(a)āᶜala to the 1st vowelled radical š following it:

An example is Form VI *tašāğara* "to be embroiled" that becomes after the assimilation *ᵓiššāğara* (cf. Howell, IV, fasc. II, 1829). The vowelled alveolar and surd *t* prefix, the *ta,* is assimilated to the vowelled pre-palatal and surd 1st radical *š,* the *ša*, resulting in *ššāğara* and the prosthetic hamza vowelled by a kasra, the *ᵓi,* is prefixed to prevent beginning the word with a vowelless segment.

8- The assimilation of the vowelled prefixed t of Form V tafaᶜᶜala or Form VI taf(a)āᶜala to the 1st vowelled radical ṣ following it:

An example is Form VI *taṣ(a)ābara* "to bear patiently" that becomes after the assimilation *ᵓiṣṣ(a)ābara* (cf. Howell, IV, fasc. II, 1829, Lane, II, 1643). The vowelled alveolar and surd *t* prefix, the *ta,* is assimilated to the vowelled dental and covered 1st radical *ṣ,* the *ṣa,* resulting in *ṣṣ(a)ābara* and the prosthetic hamza vowelled by a kasra, the *ʾi,* is prefixed to prevent beginning the word with a vowelless segment.

9- The assimilation of the vowelled prefixed t of Form V tafaʿʿala or Form VI taf(a)āʿala to the 1st vowelled radical ḍ following it:

An example is Form VI *taḍ(a)āraba* "to fight" that becomes after the assimilation *ʾiḍḍ(a)āraba* (cf. Howell, IV, fasc. II, 1829). The vowelled alveolar and surd *t* prefix, the *ta,* is assimilated to the alveolar and covered vowelled 1st radical *ḍ,* the *ḍa,* resulting in *ḍḍ(a)āraba* and the prosthetic hamza vowelled by a kasra, the *ʾi,* is prefixed to prevent beginning the word with a vowelless segment.

10- The assimilation of the vowelled prefixed t of Form V tafaʿʿala or Form VI taf(a)āʿala to the 1st vowelled radical ṭ following it:

An example is Form V *taṭahhara* "to purify one's-self" that becomes after the assimilation *ʾiṭṭahhara* (cf. Åkesson, *Ibn Masʿūd* 202: fol. 21a, Howell, IV, fasc. II, 1829, Lane, II, 1887, Penrice, *Dictionary* 91). The vowelled alveolar and surd *t* prefix, the *ta,* is assimilated to the vowelled alveolar and covered 1st radical *ṭ,* the *ṭa,* resulting in *ṭṭahhara* and the prosthetic hamza vowelled by a kasra, the *ʾi,* is prefixed to prevent beginning the word with a vowelless segment.

Another example is Form V *taṭayyara* "to see an evil omen" that becomes after the assimilation *ᵓiṭṭayyara* originally (cf. Howell, IV, fasc. II, 1829, Wright, II, 65). I can mention that the 1st person of the pl. *ᵓiṭṭayyarnā* occurs in the sur. 27: 47 *(qālū ṭṭayyarnā bi-ka wa-bi-man maᶜaka)* "They said: [1] omen do we augur from thee and those that are with thee".

11- The assimilation of the vowelled prefixed t of Form V tafaᶜᶜala or Form VI taf(a)āᶜala to the 1st vowelled radical ẓ following it:

An example is Form VI *taẓ(a)ālama* "to wrong" that becomes after the assimilation *ᵓiẓẓ(a)ālama* (cf. Howell, IV, fasc. II, 1829). The vowelled alveolar and surd *t* prefix, the *ta,* is assimilated to the vowelled interdental and covered 1st radical *ẓ,* the *ẓa,* resulting in *iẓẓ(a)ālama* and the prosthetic hamza, the *ᵓi,* is prefixed to prevent beginning the word with a vowelless segment.

1.4.2.1.2. The assimilation of the infixed vowelled t of the imperfect of Form VIII yaftaᶜilu to the vowelled 2nd radical:

The alveolar and surd infixed *t* of Form VIII can be assimilated to one of the nine segments following it (cf. Åkesson, *Ibn Masᶜūd* 200: fol. 20b, Wright, II, 64-65) that are:

1- the *t* (for the assimilation of two identical segments see par. 1.3.2.1.), 2- the alveolar and voiced *d,* 3- the interdental and voiced *ḏ,* 4- the dental, voiced and sibilant *z,* 5- the dental, surd and sibilant *s,* 6- the dental, surd and sibilant *ṣ,* 7- the alveolar and voiced *ḍ,* 8- the alveolar and voiced *ṭ,* and 9- the interdental and voiced *ẓ.* The assimilation is carried out in the imperfect of such verbs and rarely in their perfect, except in some anomalous cases as the case of *ʾiḫtaṣama* resulting in *ḥaṣṣama* (cf. Penrice, *Dictionary* 42).

The phonological procedure that is carried out in the imperfect is the following: *yaftaᶜilu* with the vowelled *t* infix following the vowelless 1st radical *f* becomes *yafatᶜilu* after that the *t's* fatḥa is shifted to the 1st radical *f.* As the *t* preceding the vowelled 2nd radical ᶜ is vowelless, it is assimilated to the ᶜ, so that it becomes *yafaᶜᶜilu.*

1- The assimilation of the vowelled infixed t of Form VIII of the imperfect yaftaᶜilu to the 2nd vowelled radical t following it in the imperfect:

This assimilation has been taken up within the sub-paragraph discussing the assimilation of two vowelled identical segments (cf. 1.3.2.1.). The example is Form VIII *yaqtatilu* "to contend among themselves" that becomes after the assimilation *yaqattilu.*

2- The assimilation of the vowelled infixed t of Form VIII of the imperfect yafta^cilu to the 2nd vowelled radical d following it:

An example is *yabtadilu* "to change" which becomes after the assimilation *yabaddilu* (cf. Åkesson, *Ibn Mas^cūd* 200: fol. 20b). The fatḥa of the *ta* in *yabtadilu* is shifted to the 1st radical *b* resulting in *yabatdilu* and the alveolar and surd *t* is assimilated to the alveolar and voiced *d,* because of their common point of articulation and because of the stronger character of the voiced segment in relation to the surd segment (for the segments see 1.2.) resulting in *yabaddilu.*

Another example of Form VIII verb with 2nd radical *d* in the imperfect is *yahtadī* that becomes after the assimilation *yahiddī* "he finds guidance" with the *h* vowelled by a kasra instead of a fatḥa. It occurs in the sur. 10: 35 *(ʾaman lā yahiddī)* "Or he who finds not guidance (himself)". Abū ^cAmr and Nāfi^c read it with both vowelless segments, the *h* and the *d,* combined, namely *yahddī,* which is disapproved by the majority, and Abū Bakr read it with both the *y* and the *h* being vowelled by a kasra, namely *yihiddī* (cf. Howell, IV, fasc. II, 1807-1808).

3- The assimilation of the vowelled infixed t of Form VIII of the imperfect yafta^cilu to the vowelled 2nd radical d following it:

An example is *ya^ctaḏiru* "to excuse one's-self" which becomes after the assimilation *ya^caḏḏiru* (cf. Åkesson, *Ibn*

Masᶜūd 200: fol. 20b). The fatḥa of the *ta* in *yaᶜtaḏiru* is shifted to the 1st radical ᶜ resulting in *yaᶜatḏiru* and the alveolar and surd *t* is assimilated to the interdental and voiced *ḏ* resulting in *yaᶜaḏḏiru.*

4- The assimilation of the vowelled infixed t of Form VIII of the imperfect yaftaᶜilu to the vowelled 2nd radical z following it:

An example is *yantaziᶜu* "to snatch, tear away" which becomes after the assimilation *yanazziᶜu* (cf. ibid). The fatḥa of the *ta* in *yantaziᶜu* is shifted to the 1st radical *n* resulting in *yanatziᶜu* and the surd *t* is assimilated to the dental, voiced and sibilant *z* resulting in *yanazziᶜu.*

5- The assimilation of the vowelled infixed t of Form VIII of the imperfect yaftaᶜilu to the vowelled 2nd radical s following it:

An example is *yabtasimu* "to smile" which becomes after the assimilation *yabassimu* (cf. ibid). The fatḥa of the *ta* in *yabtasimu* is shifted to the 1st radical *b* resulting in *yabatsimu* and the surd *t* is assimilated to the dental, surd and sibilant *s* resulting in *yabassimu.*

6- The assimilation of the vowelled infixed t of Form VIII of the imperfect yafta[c]*ilu to the vowelled 2nd radical ṣ following it:*

An example is *yaḫtaṣimu* "to argue" which becomes after the assimilation *yaḫassimu* (cf. ibid). The fatḥa of the *ta* in *yaḫtaṣimu* is shifted to the 1st radical *ḫ* resulting in *yaḫatṣimu* and the surd and soft *t* is assimilated to the surd, covered, sibilant *ṣ* resulting in *yaḫaṣṣimu.* The variant *yaḫiṣṣimu* occurs as well with the *ḫ* given a kasra instad of a fatḥa (cf. de Sacy, I, 223). The 3rd person of the masc. pl. *yaḫiṣṣimūna* occurs in the sur. 36: 49 *(wa-hum yaḫiṣṣimūna)* "While they are yet disputing among themselves!". Seven different readings are known to have been transmitted concerning the verb in this sur. (cf. Ibn Manẓūr, II, 1177 in the note), namely: 1- *yaḫṣimūna.* 2- *yaḫtaṣimūna.* 3- *yaḫiṣṣimūna.* 4- *yiḫiṣṣimūna.* 5- *yaḫaṣṣimūna.* 6- *yaḫaṣimūna.* 7- *yaḫ*[a]*ṣṣimūna* read with a vowel of support . Fleisch, *Traité I,* 142 referring to Baiḍāwī, mentions that Abū Bakr read *yiḫissimūna.* Furthermore, referring to the *Taysīr* 184, he mentions that Ibn Kaṯīr, Warš and Hišām read *yaḫaṣṣimūna,* Qālūn and Abū [c]Amr read *yaḫ*[a]*ṣṣimūna* with a vowel of support (for discussions see Fleisch, *Traité I,* 144, Cantineau, *Voyelle* 57). Ḥamza read *yaḫṣimūna* and [c]Āṣim, Ibn Ḏakwān and al-Kisā[ɔ]ī read *yaḫiṣṣimūna.* Mu[ɔ]addib, *Taṣrīf* 166 mentions that *yaḫiṣṣimūna* was read so by al-Ḥasan al-Baṣrī, *yaḫṣṣimūna* was read so by al-A[c]raǧ, Abū Ǧa[c]far and Abū [c]Amr, both *yaḫiṣṣimūna* and *yaḫaṣṣimūna* were read so by Abū [c]Amr, *yaḫṣimūna* was read so by al-A[c]maš and both *yiḫiṣṣimūna* and *yaḫtaṣimūna* were read so by other readers (see further for the different readings Ibn Muğāhid, *Sab^ca* 541, Ibn Ḫālawaihi, Qirā°āt II, 234).

7- The assimilation of the vowelled infixed t of Form VIII of the imperfect yafta^cilu to the vowelled 2nd radical ḍ following it:

An example is *yantaḍilu* "to struggle" which becomes after the assimilation *yanaḍḍilu* (cf. Åkesson, *Ibn Mas^cūd* 200: fol. 20b). The fatḥa of the *ta* in *yantaḍilu* is shifted to the 1st radical *n* resulting in *yanatḍilu* and the surd and soft *t* is assimilated to the alveolar, voiced and covered *ḍ* resulting in *yanaḍḍilu.*

8- The assimilation of the vowelled infixed t of Form VIII of the imperfect yafta^cilu to the vowelled 2nd radical ṭ following it:

An example is *yaltaṭimu* "to collide, clash" which becomes after the assimilation *yalaṭṭimu* (cf. ibid). The fatḥa of the *ta* in *yaltaṭimu* is shifted to the 1st radical *l* resulting in *yalatṭimu* and the surd and soft *t* is assimilated to the voiced and covered *ṭ* resulting in *yalaṭṭimu.*

9- The assimilation of the vowelled infixed t of Form VIII of the imperfect yaftaᶜilu to the ẓ following it:

An example is *yantaẓiru* "to expect" which becomes after the assimilation *yanaẓẓiru* (cf. ibid). The fatḥa of the *ta* in *yantaẓiru* is shifted to the 1st radical *n* resulting in *yanatẓiru* and the alveolar, surd and soft *t* is assimilated to the interdental, voiced and covered *ẓ* resulting in *yanaẓẓiru.*

1.4.2.2. The assimilation that is carried out from the 1st vowelled segment to a 2nd vowelled segment in two words following each other:

The assimilation can be carried out from a 1st vowelled segment which is the last segment of a word to a 2nd vowelled segment that is the initial segment of the word following it (for a general study see Sībawaihi, II, 455 sqq., Zamaḫšarī, 191 sqq., Cantineau, *Études* 35 sqq., Fleisch, *Traité I,* 83 sqq., Roman, *Étude I,* 390-427, Wright, I, 15-16), if both different segments originate from a common point of articulation of from close points of articulation. The following cases can be mentioned:

1- The b's assimilation to:

a) - the *m:* An example is a reading of the sur. 2: 284 *(wa-yuᶜaḏḏi(b) mman yašāʾu)* "And punisheth whom He pleaseth" (cf. Zamaḫšarī, 195, Ibn Yaᶜīš, X, 147, Vollers, *Volkssprache* 35).

<u>*2- The t's assimilation to:*</u>

a)- the *ṯ:* An example is *saka(t) ṯṯāmirun* "a wealthy man was silent" (cf. Howell, IV, fasc. II, 1795, Cantineau, *Études* 35).

b)- the *ǧ:* An example is a reading of the sur. 22: 36 *(waǧaba(t) ǧǧunūbuhā)* "When they are down on their sides (after slaughter)" (cf. Zamaḫšarī, 193, Vollers, *Volkssprache* 27).

c)- the *d:* An example is *ᵓinᶜa(t) ddulāmata* "describe Dulāmata" (cf. Ibn Yaᶜīš, X, 146, Vollers, *Volkssprache* 29).

d)- the *ḏ:* An example is a reading of the sur. 51: 1 *(wa-l-ḏārī(t) ḏḏarwan)* "By the (Winds) that scatter broadcast", read so by Ibn al-ᶜAlāᵓ and Ḥamza (cf. Vollers, *Volkssprache* 29, Cantineau, *Études* 35).

e)- the *z:* An example is *saka(t) zzāǧirun* "a diviner was silent" (cf. Howell, IV, fasc. II, 1795, Cantineau, *Études* 35).

f)- the *s,* e.g. *saka(t) ssāmirun* "a converser by night was silent" (cf. Howell, IV, fasc. II, 1795, Cantineau, *Études* 35).

g)- the *š,* e.g. *ᶜaṣaba(t) ššarban* "she obtained a drink" (cf. Ibn Yaᶜīš, X, 139, Vollers, *Volkssprache* 31).

h)- the *ṣ,* e.g. *saka(t) ṣṣābirun* "a patient man was silent" (cf. Howell, IV, fasc. II, 1795, Cantineau, *Études* 35).

i)- the *ḍ,* e.g. *šudda(t) ḍḍafāᵓiruhā* "her plaits were tightenend" (cf. Zamaḫšarī, 193).

j)- the *ṭ:* An example is *(qāla(t) ṭṭāᵓifatun* "a sect said". Another one is the reading of the sur. 4: 81 *(bayya(t) ṭṭāᵓifatun)* "a section of them meditate all night" (cf. Vollers, *Volkssprache* 32, Cantineau, *Études* 35).

k)- the ẓ, e.g. *saka(t) ẓẓālimun* "Ẓālim was silent" (cf. Howell, IV, fasc. II, 1795, Cantineau, *Études* 35).

3- The t's assimilation to:

a)- the *ḏ:* An example is a reading of the sur 3: 14 *(wa-l-ḥar(ṯ) ḏḏālika)* "And well-tilled land. Such are" (cf. Ibn ᶜUṣfūr, II, 722).

4- The ǧ's assimilation to:

a) – the *t:* An example is the saying by al-Yazīdī concerning the reading of Abū ᶜAmr of the sur. 70: 3-4 *(ḏī l-maᶜāri(ǧ)* *tta^cruğ)* "Lord of the Ways of Ascent. [The angels and the Spirit] ascend" (cf. Zamaḫšarī, 193, Ibn Ya^cīš, X, 138, Ibn ^cUṣfūr, II, 722, Vollers, *Volkssprach*e 26).

b)- the *š:* An example is a reading of the sur. 48: 29 *(ʾaḫra(ğ) ššaṭʾahu)* "Which sends forth its blade" (cf. Zamaḫšarī, 193, Åkesson, *Ibn Mas^cūd* 194: fol. 17b).

The sentence is written in Arabic as *ʾaḫrağ ššaṭʾahu* (أَخْرَجْ شّطْأَهُ) with the *ğ*, which is the last segment of the first word, deprived of a vowel or of a sukūn, and with the *š,* which is the initial segment of the second word, given a *šadda* as an indication of the assimilation of the *ğ* to it.

Another example is *ʾaḫri(ğ) ššabaṯan* "expel Šabaṯ" (cf. ibid, 193, Ibn Ya^cīš, X, 138, Vollers, Volkssprache 32).

5- The ḥ's assimilation to:

a)- the ^c: An example is a reading of the sur. 3: 185 *(fa-man zuḥzi(ḥ) ^{cc}ani l-nāri)* "Only he who is saved far from the Fire", read so by Abū ^cAmr as al-Yazīdī said about him (cf. Zamaḫšarī, 192, Ibn Ya^cīš, X, 136, Ibn ^cUṣfūr, II, 722, Vollers, *Volkssprache* 33).

6- The d's assimilation to:

a)- the *t:* An example is a reading of the sur. 16: 91 *(wa-lā tanquḍū l-ʾaymāna ba^c(d) ttawkīdihā)* "And break not your oaths after ye have confirmed them", read so by Abū ᶜAmr (cf. Ibn ᶜUṣfūr, II, 723).

b)- the *ṣ:* An example is a reading of the sur. 19: 29 *(al-mah(d) ṣṣibīyyan)* "a child in the craddle", read so by Abū ᶜAmr (cf. Ibn ᶜUṣfūr, II, 723).

c)- the *ḍ:* An example is a reading of the sur. 41: 50 *(massathu min baᶜ(d) ḍḍarrāʾa)* "After some adversity has touched him".

7- The d's assimilation to:

a)- the ǧ: An example is a reading of the sur. 33: 10 *(ʾi(ḏ) ǧǧāʾukum)* "Behold! they came on you" (cf. Zamaḫšarī, 193, Vollers, *Volkssprache* 27).

8- The r's assimilation to:

a)- the *l:* An example is a reading of the sur. 3: 147 *(ġfi(r) llanā)* "Forgive us", sur. 9: 80 *(ʾistaġfi(r) llahum)* "Whether thou ask for their forgiveness", the sur. 61: 12 *(yaġfi(r) llakum ḏunūbakum)* "He will forgive you your sins", all read so by Abū ᶜAmr as mentioned by Abū Bakr b. Muǧāhid (cf. Ibn Yaᶜīš, X, 143, Ibn ᶜUṣfūr, II, 724), - However, according to Vollers, *Volkssprache* 35 the last sur. is read so by Yaᶜqūb al-Ḥaḍrami - ; the sur. 11: 78 *(hunna ʾaṭha(r) llakum)* "They are purer for you (if ye marry)!" and the sur. 22: 65 *(ṣaḫḫa(r) llakum)* "Has made subject to you (men)" (cf. Ibn Yaᶜīš, X, 143, Vollers, *Volkssprache* 35).

9- The s's assimilation to:

a)- the *š:* An example is a reading of the sur. 19: 4 *(ʾiǧtaᶜala l-raʾ(s) ššayban)* "And the hair of my head doth glisten with grey", read so by Abū ᶜAmr (cf. Ibn Yaᶜīš, X, 139, Ibn ᶜUṣfūr, II, 726).

10- The š's assimilation to:

a)- the *s:* An example is a reading of the sur. 71: 16 *(ʾal-šam(s) ssirāǧan)* "[And made] the sun as a (Glorious) Lamp", read so by Abū ᶜAmr (cf. Ibn ᶜUṣfūr, II, 725).

11- The ḍ's assimilation to:

a)- the *š:* An example is a reading of the sur. 24: 62 *li-baᶜ(ḍ) ššaʾnihim),* read so by Abū ᶜAmr (cf. Zamaḫšarī, 193, Ibn ᶜUṣfūr, II, 725, Vollers, *Volkssprache* 31).

12- The f's assimilation to:

a)- the *b:* An example is a reading of the sur. 34: 9 *(naḫsi(f) bbihim)* "We could cause the earth to swallow them up", read so only by al-Kisāʾī and is considered weak (cf. Zamaḫšarī, 195, Ibn Yaᶜīš, X, 146, Ibn ᶜUṣfūr, II, 720, Vollers, *Volkssprache* 25).

13- The q's assimilation to:

a)- the *k*: An example is a reading of the sur. 24: 45 *(ḫala(q) kkulla dābbatin)* "Has created every animal" (cf. Zamaḫšarī, 193, Ibn Yaᶜīš, X, 138, Vollers, *Volkssprache* 34).

14- The k's assimilation to:

a)- the *q:* An example is a reading of the sur. 47: 18 *(ʾiḏā ḫarağū min ᶜinda(k) qqālū)* "When they go out from thee, they say" (cf. Zamaḫšarī, 193, Ibn Yaᶜīš, X, 138, Vollers, *Volkssprache* 34).

15- The l's assimilation to:

a)- the *t:* An example is a reading of the sur. 2: 170 *(ba(l) ttattabiᶜu mā ʾalqaynā)* "Nay! we shall follow the ways" (cf. Ibn Yaᶜīš, X, 142).

b)- the *r:* An example is a reading of the sur. 89: 6 *(kay(f) ffaᶜa(l) rrabbuka)* "How thy Lord dealt" (cf. Zamaḫšarī, 194, Ibn Yaᶜīš, X, 143).

16- The m's assimilation to:

a)- the *b:* An example is a reading of the sur. 4: 156 *(marya(m) bbuhtānan)* "Mary [a grave] false charge", the sur. 6: 53 *bi-ʾaᶜla(m) bbi-l-ššākirīna)* "[Does not God] know best those who are grateful?" and the sur. 16: 70 *(li-kaylā yaᶜla(m) bbaᶜda ᶜilmin šayʾan)* "So that they know nothing after having known (much)", read so by Abū ᶜAmr (cf. Ibn Yaᶜīš, X, 147, Ibn ᶜUṣfūr, II, 719).

17- The n's assimilation to:

a)- the *r:* An example is a reading of the sur. 7: 167 *(wa-ʾiḏ taʾaḏ(n) rrabbukum)* "Behold! thy Lord did declare" (cf. Zamaḫšarī, 194, Ibn Yaᶜīš, X, 143).

b)- the *l:* An example is a reading of the sur. 2: 133 *(wa-naḥ(n) llahu muslimūna)* "to Him we bow (in Islam)", read so by Abū ᶜAmr (cf. Ibn ᶜUṣfūr, II, 725).

c- the *y:* An example is a reading of the sur. 3: 129 *(yaġfiru li-ma(n) yyašāʾu)* "He forgiveth whom He pleaseth" (cf. Ibn Yaᶜīš, X, 147, Vollers, *Volkssprache* 36).

18- The h's assimilation to:

a)- the *l:* An example is a reading of the sur. 29: 26 *(fa-āma(n) llahu lūṭun)* "But Lūṭ had faith in Him" (cf. Ibn Yaᶜīš, X, 143).

2. THE SUBSTITUTION

The substitution is usually carried out in a word in order to alleviate the pronunciation if there exists in it a combination of two sounds which is deemed as heavy, or if both these segments' points of articulation are close to each other, or if the segments are akin in character (for the segments see par. 1.2). Other more unusual reasons relate to the peculiarity of a dialectal variant, to a verse's metrical exigency or to the exigency of the pause.

2.1. The segments of substitution

There exist special segments which are recognized as segments that can be substituted for other segments (for a study of the substitution see Ibn Ǧinnī, *de Flexione* 19-30, Ibn ᶜUṣfūr, I, 319-415, Zamaḫšarī, 172-177, Ibn Yaᶜīš, X, 7-54, Howell, IV, fasc. I, 1182-1203). These segments are termed as *ḥurūf al-ibdāl* "segments of substitution". They are comprised in different phrases, among them *ᵓistanǧadahu yawma ṣāla Ẓuṭṭa* "he asked him for help on the day some Zuṭṭ [sc. a race of Hindus] attacked" (cf. Zamaḫšarī, 172, Ibn Yaᶜīš, X, 7-8, Åkesson, *Ibn Masᶜūd* 330, fol. 33b, Howell, IV, fasc. I, 1192-1193), which starts with the ᵓ and ends with the *ṭ*. According to their order in this phrase these segments are: 1- the ᵓ, 2- the *s*, 3- the *t*, 4- the *n*, 5- the *ǧ*, 6- the *d*, 7- the *h*, 8- the *y*, 9- the *w*, 10- the *m*, 11- the *ṣ*, 12- the *ā*, 13- the *l*, 14- the *ẓ*, and 15- the *ṭ*.

2.1.1. The substitution of the hamza

The ᵓ can be substituted for the following segments: 1- the alif of feminization, 2- the *w*, 3- the *y*, 4- the *h*, 5- the *ā* and 6- the ᶜ.

2.1.1.1. The substitution of the hamza for the alif of feminization, the ā (alif maqṣūra):

An example is *ṣaḥr(a)āᵓ* in which the hamza is substituted for the alif of feminization (cf. Ibn Ǧinnī, *de Flexione* 25, *Sirr I,*

83-84, Ibn ᶜUṣfūr, I, 329-331, Zamaḫšarī, 172, Ibn Yaᶜīš, X, 9, Åkesson, *Ibn Masᶜūd* 330: fol. 33b, Howell, IV, fasc. I, 1205). The base form *is ṣahr(a)āā* with a final *alif maqṣūra* preceded by an *alif mamdūda,* suggesting a forbidden combination of two vowelless segments, namely the *alif mamdūda* and the *alif maqṣūra*. The reason of replacing the *alif maqṣūra* by a hamza is to prevent this combination.

2.1.1.2. The substitution of the hamza for the w:

The *w* that is substituted by the hamza can be vowelled by any of the three vowels: the fatḥa, the ḍamma or the kasra.

1- The hamza vowelled by a fatḥa:

An example is *ᵓawāṣilu* (cf. Zamaḫšarī, 172, Ibn Yaᶜīš, X, 10, Ibn ᶜAqīl, II, 552, Åkesson, *Ibn Masᶜūd* 330: fol. 34a, Howell, IV, fasc. I, 1218-1222, Fleisch, *Traité I,* 152, ᶜAbd al-Tawwāb, *Taṭawwur* 41), the pl. of *wāṣilatun* "joining", that is conformable to the measure *fawāᶜilu,* in which the *ᵓa* is necessarily substituted for the 1st radical *w* vowelled by a fatḥa, the *wa,* of the base form *wawāṣilu.* The *wa* is changed into an *ᵓa* to prevent the heavy combination of both the wāws.

Another example is the imperative *ʾaḥḥid ʾaḥḥid* in which the *ʾa* is substituted for the 1st radical *w* vowelled by a fatḥa, the *wa,* of the base form *waḥḥid waḥḥid* "make the sign with one, one" (cf. Rāzī in Ḫalīl b. Aḥmad ..., *Ḥurūf* 137 in the note, Zamaḫšarī, 172, Ibn Yaᶜīš, X, 14-15, Ibn Manẓūr, VI, 4782, Åkesson, *Ibn Masᶜūd* 330: fol. 34a, Howell, IV, fasc. I, 1230). A tradition relates that Muḥammad has said this phrase to a man when he saw him making the sign with his two forefingers in reciting the creed.

2- *The hamza vowelled by a ḍamma:*

An example is *ʾuǧūhun* (cf. Sībawaihi, II, 341, Ibn Ǧinnī, *de Flexione* 25, *Sirr I,* 92, Ibn ᶜUṣfūr, I, 332, Zamaḫšarī, 172, Ibn Yaᶜīš, X, 10-11, Åkesson, *Ibn Masᶜūd* 330: fol. 34a, Howell, IV, fasc. I, 1224-1225), the pl. of *waǧhun* "face" from *waǧuha* "to be a man of distinction" which is a verb with 1st radical *w.* In *ʾuǧ(u)ūhun* the *ʾu* is possibly substituted for the 1st radical *w* vowelled by a ḍamma, the *wu,* of the base form *wuǧ(u)ūhun.* The reason of this substitution is the dislike of having the *w* vowelled by a ḍamma (cf. Sībawaihi, II, 391), which is deemed as heavy.

Another example is *ʾadʾurun* "houses" (cf. Sībawaihi, II, 341, Ibn Ǧinnī, *Sirr I,* 98, *de Flexione* 25, Zamaḫšarī, 172, Ibn ᶜUṣfūr, I, 335-336, Ibn Yaᶜīš, X, 10-11, Åkesson, *Ibn Masᶜūd* 330: fol. 34a, Howell, IV, fasc. I, 1224-1225), the pl. of *d(a)ārun,* in which the *ʾu* is necessarily substituted for the 2nd radical *w* that is vowelled by a ḍamma, the *wu,* of the base form *ʾadwurun.*

Another example is *kisāʾun* "a wrapper" in which the *ʾu* is necessarily substituted for the 3rd radical *w* (cf. Zamaḫšarī, 172, Ibn Yaᶜīš, X, 9-10, Åkesson, *Ibn Masᶜūd* 330: fol. 34a, Howell, IV, fasc. I, 1203-1204, Mokhlis, *Taṣrīf* 195) that is vowelled by a ḍamma, the *wu,* of the base form *kisāwun.* This substitution is carried out to prevent that the original *w* becomes vowelled by any of the three vowels marking the declension, namely *kisāwun* for the nominative, *kisāwan* for the accusative and *kisāwin* for the genitive, which is deemed as heavy (cf. Åkesson, *Ibn Masᶜūd* 330: fol. 34a).

3- The hamza vowelled by a kasra:

An example is *ʾišāḥun* "baldric" in which the *ʾi* is possibly substituted for the 1st radical *w* (cf. Sībawaihi, II, 341) that is vowelled by a kasra, the *wi,* of the base form *wišāḥun.*

Zamaḫšarī, 172-173 notes that al-Māzinī considered this substitition of the *w* vowelled by the kasra as *qiyās* "analogy".

Another example is the active participle *q(a)ā*ʾ*ilun* "saying" underlyingly *q(a)āwilun* from the verb *q(a)āla* "to say" underlyingly *qawala* with 2nd radical *w*. In it, the ʾ*i* is necessarily substituted for the 2nd radical *w* vowelled by a kasra, the *wi* (cf. Zamaḫšarī, 172, 180, Ibn Yaᶜīš, X, 10, Ibn ᶜUṣfūr, I, 327-329, Åkesson, *Ibn Mas*ᶜ*ūd* 330: fol. 34a, Howell, IV, fasc. I, 1209-1210, Åkesson, *Complexity* par. 6.5.9.1., par. 9.1.14.).

2.1.1.3. The substitution of the hamza for the y:

The hamza can be substituted for the *y* vowelled by a fatḥa or with a kasra.

1- The hamza vowelled by a fatḥa:

An example is ʾ*adayhi* in which the ʾ is possibly substituted for the initial *y* vowelled by a fatḥa of the base form *yadayhi* "his hands" (cf. Zamaḫšarī, 173, Ibn Yaᶜīš, X, 15, Ibn Manẓūr, VI, 4951, Åkesson, *Ibn Mas*ᶜ*ūd* 330: fol. 34a, Vernier, I 346). According to Ibn Masᶜūd (Åkesson, *Ibn Mas*ᶜ*ūd* 330: fol. 34a), the reason of this substitution is the heaviness of the fatḥa vowelling the *y*.

<u>*2- The hamza vowelled by a kasra:*</u>

An example is the active participle *b(a)ā*ʾ*i*ᶜ*un* "selling" (cf. Zamaḫšarī, 172, 180, Ibn Yaᶜīš, X, 10, Ibn ᶜUṣfūr, I, 327-329, Åkesson, *Ibn Mas*ᶜ*ūd* 330: fol. 34a, Howell, IV, fasc. I, 1209-1210, Mokhlis, *Taṣrīf* 195), from the verb *b(a)ā*ᶜ*a* "to sell" underlyingly *baya*ᶜ*a* with 2nd radical *y*. The ʾ is necessarily substituted for the 2nd radical *y* vowelled by a kasra of the base form *b(a)āyi*ᶜ*un* (cf. Åkesson, *Complexity* par. 6.5.9.2., par. 9.1.14.).

<u>*2.1.1.4. The substitution of the hamza for the h:*</u>

An example is *mā*ʾ*un* in which the ʾ is substituted for the 3rd radical *h* of the base form *māhun* "water" (cf. Ibn Ǧinnī, *Sirr I,* 100-101, Ibn ᶜUṣfūr, I, 348-351, Zamaḫšarī, 173, Ibn Yaᶜīš, X, 15-16, Åkesson, *Ibn Mas*ᶜ*ūd* 330: fol. 34a, Howell, IV, fasc. I, 1232-1235), from *mawaha* "to mix", a verb with 2nd radical *w*. The pl. form of *mā*ʾ*un* is *miyāhun* with the 3rd radical *h* and its diminutive is *muwayhun* (cf. Ibn Manẓūr, VI, 4302).

Another pl. form is *ʾamwāhun* in which the *h* is as well substituted by the *ʾ* so that it became *ʾamwāʾun.* The reason of this substitution is the oneness of the point of articulation of the *ʾ* and the *h* as they both originate from the farthest part of the throat, and are laryngals (for the segments see par. 1.2.1.). The example *ʾamwāʾuhā* occurs in this verse cited by Ibn Ǧinnī, *Sirr I,* 100, *Munṣif II,* 151, Zamaḫšarī, 173, Ibn Yaʿīš, X, 15, Ibn ʿUṣfūr, I, 348, Ibn Manẓūr, VI, 4302, Howell, IV, fasc. I, 1233, Åkesson, *Ibn Masʿūd* 347: (325)):

> *"Wa-baldatin qāliṣatin ʾamwāʾuhā*
> *māṣiḥatin raʾda l-ḍuḥā ʾafyāʾuhā".*
> "And many a land, whose waters were exhausted,
> and whose shades were passing away in the part of
> the noon when the sun was hight".

2.1.1.5. The substitution of the hamza for the ā:

An example is the active participle of Form VIII *l-muštaʾiq* (in pause) in which the *ʾi* is substituted for the *ā* of *l-muštāq* "the yearner" from *šawaqa* "to desire", a verb with 2nd radical *w,* that occurs in a verse cited by Ibn Ǧinnī, *Sirr I,* 91, *Ḫaṣāʾiṣ III,* 145, Zamaḫšarī, 172, Ibn Yaʿīš, X, 12-13, Ibn Manẓūr, II,

1405, IV, 2361, Howell, IV, fasc. I, 1227, Åkesson, *Ibn Masᶜūd* 347: (326)):

> "*Yā dāra Mayya bi-l-dakādīki l-buraq*
> *ṣabran fa-qad hayyağti šawqa l-muštaᵓiq*".
> "O abode of Mayya [sc. a woman's name] in the low-lying sands, sands mixed with stones and earth,
> give me patience, for you have excited the yearning of the yearner".

2.1.1.6. The substitution of the hamza for the ᶜ:

An example is the substantive *ᵓubābun* in which the ᵓ is substituted for the ᶜ of the base form *ᶜubābun* "billow". The reason of this substitution is the closeness of the points of articulation of the ᵓ and the ᶜ as the ᵓ originates from the farthest part of the throat and is a laryngal and the ᶜ originates from the middle of the throat and is a pharyngal (for the segments see par. 1.2.). This theory about the substitution that concerns *ᵓubābun* is however criticized by Ibn Ğinnī, *Sirr I,* 106, who does not consider the ᵓ to be substituted for the ᶜ, but that the form is *fuᶜālun,* namely *ᵓub(a)ābun* from *ᵓabba* "to prepare itself". His remark is also mentioned by Ibn Manẓūr, I, 4. The example *ᵓubābu* occurs in this verse cited by Ibn Ğinnī, *Sirr I,* 106,

Zamaḫšarī, 173, Ibn Yaᶜīš, X, 15, Ibn ᶜUṣfūr, I, 352, Howell, IV, fasc. I, 1235, Åkesson, *Ibn Masᶜūd* 349: (328):

> *"Wa-māǧa sāᶜātin malā l-wadīqi*
> *ᵓubābu baḥrin ḍāḥikin zahūqi"*
> "And the deserts of intense heats were agitated at
> times,
> like a billow of a laughing, far-extending sea".

2.1.2. The substitution of the *s*

The *s* can be substituted for the *t*.

2.1.2.1. The substitution of the s for the t:

An example is *ᵓistaḫaḏa* in which the *s* is substituted for the *t* of the base form Form VIII *ᵓittaḫaḏa* "to take for one's self" (cf. Sībawaihi, II, 480, Åkesson, *Ibn Masᶜūd* 330: fol 34a, Howell, IV, fasc. I, 1192), from *ᵓaḫaḏa* "to take". The verb *ᵓistaḫaḏa* referring to Form VIII should not be confounded with Form X *ᵓistaḫaḏa* which looks exactly the same as it. The reason why the *t* is changed into the *s* in it is that they both are among the surd segments (for them see par. 1.2.2.).

2.1.3. The substitution of the *t*

The *t* can be substituted for the following segments: 1- the *w*, 2- the *y*, 3- both the *d* and the *s*, 4- the *ṣ* and 5- the *b*.

2.1.3.1. The substitution of the t for the w:

This substitution can affect the initial segment or the ultimate segment of a word.

An example that concerns the initial segment is *tuḫamatun* in which the *t* is substituted for the initial *w* of the base form *wuḫamatun* "a malady like cholera" (cf. Ibn Yaᶜīš, X, 37-38, Åkesson, *Ibn Masᶜūd* 330: fol 34a). Some other examples (for them see Ibn Yaᶜīš, X, 38-39) are *tuǧāha* "in front of" for *wuǧāha, tayqūrun* for *wayqūrun* "grave", *tuklānun* for *wuklānun* "incapacity and reliance upon others", *tukalatun* for *wukalatun* "a man incapable, committing his affair to another", *tuhamatun* for *wuhamatun* "suspicion", *taqīyatun* for *waqīyatun* "fear", *turāṯun* for *wurāṯun* "inheritance" that occurs in the sur. 89:19 *(wa-taᵓkulūna l-turāṯa ᵓaklan lammā)* "And ye devour Inheritance - All with greed" and *tilādun* for *wilādun* "old property, what was born in your possession".

An example that concerns the ultimate segment of the word is *ʾuḫtun* "sister" in which the *t* is substituted for the 3rd radical *w* of the base form *ʾuḫwun* (cf. Zamaḫšarī, 175, Ibn Yaʿīš, X 39-40, Åkesson, *Ibn Masʿūd* 330: fol 34b, Howell, I, fasc. III, 1370-1372, IV, fasc. I, 1347-1348, ʿAbd al-Tawwāb, *Taṭawwur* 91), that is from the root *ʾa ḫ w* with 3rd radical *w*.

2.1.3.2. The substitution of the t for the y:

An example is *ṯintāni* in which the t is substituted for the 3rd radical *y* of *ṯanayānī* "the second to the one" (cf. Zamaḫšarī, 175, Ibn Yaʿīš, X, 40, Ibn ʿUṣfūr, I, 388, Åkesson, *Ibn Masʿūd* 330-332: fol 34b, Howell, IV, fasc. I, 1349-1350), from the expression *ṯanaytu l-wāḥida* "I was a second to the one", and in Form IV *ʾasnatū* for *ʾasnayū* "they experienced drough or barrenness" with 3rd radical *y*. Referring to *ʾasnatū,* Sībawaihi, II, 341 notes that the substitution of the *t* for the *y* as a 3rd radical is rare. It can be mentioned that *ṯintāni* is used in the dialectal variant of Tamīm (cf. Daqir, *Muʿǧam* 2 in the notes, 338) and *ʾiṯnāni* and *ʾiṯnatāni* are used by the Ḥiǧāzīs (cf. ibid 338). The reason of this substitution is to avoid vowelling the *y* (cf. Åkesson, *Ibn Masʿūd* 332: fol 34b), which is deemed as heavy.

2.1.3.3. The substitution of the t for the d and the s:

An example is *sittun* "six" in which the doubled *t* is substituted for the *d* and the *s* of the base form *sudusun* (cf. Sībawaihi, II, 479, Åkesson, *Ibn Mas*ᶜ*ūd* 332: fol. 34b, Zamaḫšarī, 175, 196). This substitution of the *t* for both the *d* and the *s* in *sudusun* is considered as rare by Sībawaihi, II, 341.

Other examples in which the *t* is substituted for the *s* are *l-nāti,* underlyingly *l-nāsi,* and *ʾakyāti* underlyingly *ʾakyāsi* which occur in these verses, which are believed to have been said by ᶜIlbāʾ b. Arqam al-Yaškarī. This substitution pertains to a dialectal variant that is known to be of the usage of the Yemenites, and is called *al-watmu.* The verses are cited by Rāzī in Ḫalīl b. Aḥmad ..., *Ḥurūf* 150, Ibn Fāris, *Ṣāḥibī* 109, Ibn Ǧinnī, *Sirr I,* 155, *Ḫaṣāʾiṣ II,* 53, Zamaḫšarī, 175, Ibn Yaᶜīš, X, 36, Ibn ᶜUṣfūr, I, 389, Ibn Manẓūr, I, 148, Howell, IV, fasc. I, 1352-1353, Åkesson, *Ibn Mas*ᶜ*ūd* 352: (334)):

*"Yā qātala l-lāhu banī l-si*ᶜ*lāti*
*ᶜAmr b. Mas*ᶜ*ūd širāra l-nāti*
*ġayra ʾa*ᶜ*iffāʾa wa-lā ʾakyāti"*.
"O [my people] God slay the sons of she-devils,
ᶜAmr b. Masᶜūd, the worst of men,
incontinent and not sharp-witted!".

2.1.3.4. The substitution of the t for the ṣ:

An example is *liṣtun* or *luṣtun* in which the *t* is substituted anomalously for the 2nd *ṣ* of the doubled ṣāds of the base form *liṣṣun* or *luṣṣun* "robber" (cf. Zamaḫšarī, 175, Ibn Yaᶜīš, X, 41, Åkesson, *Ibn Masᶜūd* 332: fol 34b, Howell, IV, fasc. I, 1353). The reason of this substitution is that both the *t* and the *ṣ* are among the surd segments (for the segments' characters see par. 1.2.2.), which facilitates the substitution of one for the other.

2.1.3.5. The substitution of the t for the b:

An example is *ḏaᶜālitun* in which the *t* is substituted for the *b* of the base form *ḏaᶜālibun* "worn-out rags". The example *ḏaᶜālitin* in the genitive occurs in this verse, which according to Ibn Manẓūr, II, 1504, 2100, is said by one of the Banū ᶜAwf b. Saᶜd. It is also cited by Ibn Ǧinnī, *Sirr I,* 157, Howell, IV, fasc. I, 1355, Åkesson, *Ibn Masᶜūd* 353: (336):

> *"Ṣafqatu ḏī ḏaᶜālitin samūli*
> *bayᶜu mriʾin laysa bi-mustaqīli"*
> "The bargain of the poor needy purchaser, wearer
> of worn-out rags is, in irrevocability and
> conclusiveness,

like a sale by a man that is not desirous of
rescinding".

2.1.4. The substitution of the *n*

The *n* can be substituted for the following segments: 1- the *w* and 2- the *l*.

2.1.4.1. The substitution of the n for the w:

An example is *ṣanᶜānīyu* "someone or something from a city in Yemen" in which the *n* is substituted for the *w* of the base form *ṣanᶜāwīyu* (cf. Ibn Ǧinnī, *de Flexione* 25-26, *Sirr II,* 441, Zamaḫšarī, 175, Ibn Yaᶜīš, X, 36, Ibn ᶜUṣfūr, I, 395-396, Howell, IV, fasc. I, 1335-1336), which is the relative noun of *ṣanᶜāʾu* "a city in Yemen".

2.1.4.2. The substitution of the n for the l:

The *n* in *laᶜanna* is substituted for the *l* of the base form *laᶜalla* "maybe" (cf. Ibn Ǧinnī, *Sirr II,* 442, Zamaḫšarī, 175, Ibn Yaᶜīš, X, 36, Ibn ᶜUṣfūr, I, 395, Howell, IV, fasc. I, 1336-1337).

2.1.5. The substitution of the ǧ

The *ǧ* can be substituted for the *y*.

2.1.5.1. The substitution of the ǧ for the y:

The *ǧ* is substituted for the single *y*, but less often than the double one in pause. Examples referring to the single *y* are *ḥaǧǧatiǧ* underlyingly *ḥaǧǧatiy* "my pilgrimage" (that results in *ḥaǧǧat(i)ī* after the assimilation of the *y* to the *i)* and *biǧ* for *biy* "me" (that results in *b(i)ī* after the assimilation of the *y* to the *i),* which occur in this verse, whose author is, according to the editor of Ibn al-Sarrāǧ, *Uṣūl III,* 274, Abū Zaid: Saᶜīd b. Aus b. Ṯābit al-Anṣārī, the author of *al-Nawādir.* It is also cited by Ibn Ǧinnī, *Sirr I,* 177, *de Flexione* 30, Zamaḫšarī, 176, Ibn Yaᶜīš, X, 50, *Mulūkī* 329, Ibn ᶜUṣfūr, I, 355, Howell, IV, fasc. I, 1376, Lane, I, 47, Vernier, I, 356-357, Åkesson, *Ibn Masᶜūd* 354: (340):

> *"Lāhumma ᵓin kunta qabilta ḥaǧǧatiǧ*
> *fa-lā yazālu šāḥiǧun yaᵓtīka biǧ".*
> "O God, if You have accepted my pilgrimage,
> then a mule shall not cease to bring me to You".

Examples that refer to the doubled *y* are ᶜ*Aliǧǧi* "ᶜAlī" in which the double ǧ is substituted for the double *y* of ᶜ*Aliyyi* in the construct state ᵓ*Abū* ᶜ*Aliǧǧi* "Abū ᶜAlī" of the verse cited below, and *bi-l-*ᶜ*ašiǧǧi* said instead of bi-l-ᶜašiyyi in it. This phenomenon pertains to the dialectal variant of Quḍāᶜa, Banū Tamīm and Banū Saᶜd, and is known as *al-*ᶜ*aǧ*ᶜ*aǧa*. Both these words occur in this verse said by an inhabitant of the desert, cited by Sībawaihi, II, 315, Ibn Fāris, *Ṣāḥibī* 55, Ibn Ǧinnī, *Sirr I*, 175, de Flexione 30, Ibn al-Sarrāǧ, *Uṣūl III*, 274, Zamaḫšarī, 176, Ibn Yaᶜīš, X 50, *Mulūkī* 248, 329, 330, Ibn ᶜUṣfūr, I, 353, Howell, IV, fasc. I, 1375-1376, Lane, I, 47, Vernier, I, 356, Åkesson, *Ibn Mas*ᶜ*ūd* 354: (339):

"*Ḫālī* ᶜ*Uwayfun wa-*ᵓ*Abū* ᶜ*Aliǧǧi*
ᵓ*al-muṭ*ᶜ*imānī l-laḥmi bi-l-*ᶜ*ašiǧǧi*".
"My maternal uncle ᶜUwayf and Abū ᶜAliǧǧi [sc. Abū ᶜAlī],
they who provide meat for food at evening".

2.1.6. The substitution of the *d*

The *d* can be substituted for the *t*.

2.1.6.1. The substitution of the d for the t:

An example is *fuzdu* in which the *d* is substituted for the *t* of the base form *fuztu* "I succeeded" (cf. Zamaḫšarī, 176, 196, Ibn Yaᶜīš, X, 48, 151, Åkesson, *Ibn Masᶜūd* 332: fol 34b, Howell, IV, fasc. I, 1373). The *-tu* is the suffixed agent pronoun of the 1st person of the singular and the verb is *fawaza* with middle radical *w*.

Another example is *ᵓiǧdamaᶜū* in which the *d* is substituted for the infixed *t* of the base form VIII *ᵓiǧtamaᶜū* "they gathered together" (cf. Ibn Fāris, *Ṣāḥibī* 109, Ibn Yaᶜīš, X, 49, Howell, IV, fasc. I, 1372).

2.1.7. The substitution of the *h*

The *h* can be substituted for the following segments: 1- the ᵓ, 2- the *ā*, 3- the *y* and 4- the *t*.

2.1.7.1. The substitution of the h for the hamza:

The *h* in Form I *haraqtu* "I spilled" is substituted for the ᵓ of its base form *ᵓaraqtu* (cf. Sībawaihi, II, 341, 364, Åkesson, *Ibn*

Mas^c^ūd 332: fol 34b, de Sacy, I, 247, 224 note 1, Vernier, I, 152).

2.1.7.2. The substitution of the h for the ā:

The last *h* in *ḥayyahalah* "come along!" is substituted for the *ā* of the base form constituted of two words *ḥayya halā* (cf. Zamaḫšarī, 156, 175, Ibn Ya^c^īš, X, 43, Åkesson, *Ibn Mas^c^ūd* 332: fol 34b) in pause. The other variants are *ḥayya hal* with the sukūn in pause and *ḥayya hala* otherwise (cf. Wright, II, 294). The example *ḥayyahalah* belongs to the category of words that has been determined by Sībawaihi, I, 104 as "nouns in the sing. pertaining to verbs, (whose action they denote)" (for a study see Sībawaihi, I, 105-107, Versteegh, *Zağğāğī* 63). A verse said by a man of the Banū Bakr b. Wa^ɔ^īl, cited by Zamaḫšarī, 62, Ibn Ya^c^īš, IV, 46, Ibn Manẓūr, VI, 4693, Howell, I, fasc. II, 682, Åkesson, *Ibn Mas^c^ūd* 356: (344) has *ḥayyahaluh* with the ḍamma as a vowel of declension over the *l:*

> *"Wa-hayyağa l-ḥayya min dārin fa-ẓalla lahum*
> *yawmun kaṯīrun tanādīhi wa-ḥayyahaluh.*
> "And he [sc. the camel-driver] roused the tribe
> from an abode;

and a day, in which the calling of one to another
and "make haste" were many, was spent by them".

The *h* in *ʾanah* is substituted for the *ā* of *ʾanā* "I" (cf. Ibn Ǧinnī, *Sirr I,* 163, II, 555, de Flexione 22, 28, Zamaḫšarī, 175, Ibn Yaᶜīš, III, 138, IV, 6, IX, 80-81, X, 43, Åkesson, *Ibn Masᶜūd* 332: fol 34b, Howell, I, fasc. II, 577).

2.1.7.3. The substitution of the h for the y:

The *h* that marks the fem. sing. in the demonstratif pronoun *hāḏihi* "this is" from the phrase *hāḏihi ʾamatu l-lāhi* "this is the servant of God", is substituted for the *y* of the base form *hāḏī* (cf. Rāzī, in Ḫalīl b. Aḥmad ..., *Ḥurūf* 154, Sībawaihi, II, 341, Ibn Ǧinnī, *Sirr II,* 556, Zamaḫšarī, 176, Ibn Yaᶜīš, III, 131, X, 44-45, Åkesson, *Ibn Masᶜūd* 332: fol 34b).

2.1.7.4. The substitution of the h for the t:

The *h* in Ṭalḥah "Ṭalḥa" is substituted for the *tāʾ marbūṭa* of its base form Ṭalḥat (cf. Zamaḫšarī, 176, Ibn Yaᶜīš, X, 45, Åkesson, *Ibn Masᶜūd* 332: fols. 34b-35a, Howell, IV, fasc. I, 1364-1365, Fleisch, *Traité I,* 183-184) in pause. This substitution is carried out specifically in nouns ending with the *tāʾ marbūṭa* which marks in them the fem. sing. and not in verbs that occur in the perfect of the fem. sing. ending with the suffixed *tāʾ ṭawīla* that marks the fem. sing., e.g. *ḍarabat* "she hit". It can be noted that the characteristic *tāʾ ṭawīla* suffixed to verbs cannot be substituted by the *h* in pause, i.e. *ḍarabat* cannot become *ḍarabah,* as there is a risk of confounding this *h* with the suffixed pronoun of the accusative of the 3rd person of the masc. sing., the *-hu* "him", because in the written form without vowels both *ḍarabah* and *ḍarabahu* "he hit him" would look alike, i.e. ضربه.

2.1.8. The substitution of the *y*

The *y* or the *ī* can be substituted for the following segments: 1- the *ā,* 2- the *w,* 3- the ʾ, 4- one of the doubled segments, 5- the *n,* 6- the ʿ, 7- the *t,* 8- the *b,* 9- the *s* and 10- the *ṯ.*

2.1.8.1. The substitution of the ī for the ā:

The *ī* in *mufaytīḥun* "a little key" is substituted for the *ā.* The example *mufayt(i)īḥun* is the diminutive of *miftāḥun,* and is conformable to *fuʿayʿ(i)īlun.* It is the last vowelless *ī* in this example that is considered to be substituted for the *ā* (cf. Ibn

Ǧinnī, *de Flexione* 23, *Sirr II,* 731-732, Zamaḫšarī, 173, Ibn Yaᶜīš, X, 21, Åkesson, *Ibn Masᶜūd* 332: fol 35a, Howell, IV, fasc. I, 1256) as it is preceded by a kasra. The pattern *fuᶜayᶜīlun* is appliable to every quinqueliteral noun in which the 4th segment is an *ā, ū* or ī (for examples see Zamaḫšarī, 87, Howell, I, fasc. III, 1167, Wright, II, 166, Vernier, I, 198), e.g. *miṣbāhun: muṣaybīḥun* "little lamp", *qarbūsun: quraybīsun* "a little pommel of a saddle", and *qindīlun: qunaydīlun* "little candelabrum".

2.1.8.2. *The substitution of the y for the w:*

The *y* in *miyqātun* (which results in *m(i)īqātun* after the assimilation of the *y* to the *i)* is substituted for the vowelless *w* of the base form *miwqātun* "time appointed for performance of an action" (cf. Zamaḫšarī, 173, 185, Ibn Yaᶜīš, X, 21, Åkesson, *Ibn Masᶜūd* 332: fol. 35a, Howell, IV, fasc. I, 1270-1271), because the *w* is vowelless and influenced by the kasra preceding it.

The *y* in *miyzānun* (which results in *m(i)īzānun* after the assimilation of the *y* to the *i)* is substituted for the vowelless *w* of the base form *miwzānun* "balance" (cf. Ibn Ǧinnī, *Munṣif I,* 220-221, Åkesson, *Ibn Masᶜūd* 282: fol 27a, *Complexity* par.

9.1.17.) from the root *w z n*. The reason of this substitution is the vowellessness of the *w* and the influence of the kasra preceding it.

The second *y* of the doubled yāᵓs in the noun in the sing. *kayyanūnatun* is substituted for the 2nd radical *w* vowelled by a fatḥa of the base form *kaywanūnatun* "being" which is conformable to *fayᶜalūlatun,* and then the vowelless *y* is assimilated to the *w* (cf. Ibn Ǧinnī, *Munṣif II,* 10, Åkesson, *Ibn Masᶜūd* 282: fol. 27a-27b, *Complexity* par. 9.1.12.2.). Likewise, the second of the doubled yāᵓs in the noun in the sing. *mayyitun* is substituted for the *w* vowelled by a kasra of the base form *maywitun* "a dead man", and then the vowelless *y* is assimilated to the *w* (cf. Åkesson, *Ibn Masᶜūd* 282: fol. 27b, *Complexity* par. 9.1.13.1.).

The *y* in the broken pl. *diy(a)ārun* is substituted for the 2nd radical *w* vowelled by a fatḥa of the base form *diw(a)ārun* "houses" (cf. Åkesson, *Ibn Masᶜūd* 284: fol. 28a, Howell, IV, fasc. I, 1264, Åkesson, *Complexity* par. 9.1.9.1.). Other examples are *siy(a)āṭun* in which the *y* is substituted for the 2nd radical *w* vowelled by a fatḥa of the base form *siw(a)āṭun* "whips" and the verbal noun *qiy(a)āmun* in which the *y* is substituted for the 2nd radical *w* vowelled by a fatḥa of the base form *qiw(a)āmun* "standing".

2.1.8.3. The substitution of the y for the hamza:

The vowelless *ī* in *ḏ(i)ībun* is possibly substituted for the ᵓ of the base form *ḏiᵓbun* "a wolf" (cf. Zamaḫšarī, 173, Ibn Yaᶜīš, X, 24, Åkesson, *Ibn Masᶜūd* 332: fol 35a, Howell, IV, fasc. I, 1287).

2.1.8.4. The substitution of the y for one of the doubled segments in the doubled verb:

This substitution is discussed in par. 1.3.3: 4 and par. 2.2.1.7. Some examples that are taken up there are Form V *tasarraytu* said instead of *tasarrartu* "I had a concubine" and Form V *taẓannaytu* "I formed an opinion" said instead of *taẓannantu.*

2.1.8.5. The substitution of the y for the n:

The last *y* among the doubled yāᵓs in *ᵓanāsiyyu* is substituted for the *n* (cf. Ibn Yaᶜīš, X, 27, Ibn Manẓūr, I, 148, Åkesson, *Ibn Masᶜūd* 332: fol. 35a, Howell, I, fasc. III, 100, IV, fasc. I, 1296) of the base form *ᵓanās(i)ynu* "men" that results after the assimilation of the *y* to the *i* in *ᵓanās(i)īnu.* The example *ᵓanāsiyyu* is said to be the pl. of *ᵓinsānun,* and not of *ᵓinsīyun* "a human being, man".

The y in *d(i)ynārun* is substituted for the *n* of *dinnārun* (cf. Ibn Ǧinnī, *de Flexione* 24, *Sirr II,* 757, Åkesson, *Ibn Mas^{c}ūd* 332: fol. 35a, Howell, IV, fasc. I, 1298, I, fasc. III, 1197, Wright, II, 175).

2.1.8.6. The substitution of the ī for the ^{c}:

The *ī* in *ḍafād(i)ī* is substituted for the ^{c} of the base form *ḍafādi^c* "frogs" (cf. Åkesson, *Ibn Mas^{c}ūd* 332: fol. 35a, Nöldeke, *Grammatik* 13). The ^{c} in *ḍafādi^c* is counted as heavy on account that it is a guttural segment, and as the kasra preceding it is closer to the *ī,* it became more natural to replace the ^{c} by the *ī*. The example *ḍafādī* occurs in the saying of Ḫalaf al-Aḥmar, whose verse is cited by Sībawaihi, I, 300, Ibn Ǧinnī, *Sirr II,* 762, Zamaḫšarī, 174, Ibn Ya^{c}īš, X, 28, Ibn ^{c}Uṣfūr, I, 376, Ibn Manẓūr, IV, 2594, Howell, IV, fasc. I, 1296, Åkesson, *Ibn Mas^{c}ūd* 361: (355):

> *"Wa-manhalin laysa lahu ḥawāziqu*
> *wa-li-ḍafādī ǧammihi naqāniqu".*
> "And many a watering-place, which has no sides
> preventing any one from coming down to it, but to
> which every one is able to come down from all of
> its sides,
> and the frogs of whose main part have croakings!"

2.1.8.7. The substitution of the y for the t:

The *y* in *ʾiytaṣalat* "it joined" (that results after the assimilation of the *y* to the *i* in *ʾ(i)ītaṣalat)* is substituted for the *w* (cf. Ibn Ǧinnī, *Sirr II,* 764, Ibn Yaᶜīš, X, 26, *Mulūkī* 248, Ibn ᶜUṣfūr, I, 378, Ibn Manẓūr, VI, 4850, Åkesson, *Ibn Masᶜūd* 332: fol. 35a, Howell, IV, fasc. I, 1296) of the base form VIII *ʾiwtaṣalat* "it joined" from *waṣala* "to join". The example *ʾiwtaṣalat* has a vowelless *w,* which is at first assimilated to the infixed *t* of Form VIII resulting in *ʾittaṣalat.* Then the vowelless *t* is anomalously changed into a *y* on account of the influence of the kasra preceding it resulting in *ʾiytaṣalat.* The example *fa-ytaṣalat* occurs in this verse said by an unkown poet, in which he describes a wild cow searching for her calf. It is cited by Ibn Ǧinnī, *Sirr II,* 764, Ibn Yaᶜīš, X, 26, *Mulūkī* 248, Ibn ᶜUṣfūr, I, 378, Ibn Manẓūr, VI, 4850, Howell, IV, fasc. I, 1296, Åkesson, *Ibn Masᶜūd* 362: (356):

> *"Qāmat bi-hā tanšudu kullu l-munšadi*
> *fa-ytaṣalat bi-miṯli ḍawʾi l-farqadi".*
> "She stood in it [sc. the patch of ground], seeking with all inquiry, and joined [a calf] like the light [of the asterism called] al-farqad, [by which one guides oneself]".

2.1.8.8. The substitution of the y for the b:

The y in *ṭaʿāl(i)y* (that results after the assimilation of the y to the i in *ṭaʿāl(i)ī*) is substituted for the b of *ṭaʿālib* "foxes" (cf. Åkesson, *Ibn Masʿūd* 332: fol. 35a). The reason of this substitution seems to be the influence of the kasra preceding the b. The example *l-ṭaʿālī* occurs instead of *l-ṭaʿālibi* (in the genitive) and *ʾarānīhā* instead of *ʾarānibuhā* (cf. Nöldeke, *Grammatik* 13) in this verse cited by Sībawaihi, I, 300, Ibn Ğinnī, *Sirr II*, 742, Ibn al-Sarrāğ, *Uṣūl III*, 467, Zamaḫšarī, 174, Ibn Yaʿīš, X, 24, 28, *Mulūkī* 254, Ibn ʿUṣfūr, I, 369, Howell, IV, fasc. I, 1297, Åkesson, *Ibn Masʿūd* 362: (357):

"*La-hā ʾašārīru min laḥmin tutammiruhu*
mina l-ṭaʿālī wa-waḥzun min ʾarānīhā".
"She has bits of flesh that she dries,
of foxes, and a little of her hares".

2.1.8.9. The substitution of the y for the s:

The y in *sād(i)y* (that results after the assimilation of the y to the i in *sād(i)ī*) is substituted for the s of the base form *sādis* "the sixth" (cf. Åkesson, *Ibn Masʿūd* 332: fol. 35a, Nöldeke, *Grammatik* 13). The reason of this substitution seems to be the influence of the kasra preceding the s. The example *sādī* occurs in this verse said by Imruᵓu l-Qais, cited by Ibn Ǧinnī, *Sirr II,* 741, Zamaḫšarī, 174, Ibn Yaᶜīš, X, 24, 28, *Mulūkī 255,* Ibn ᶜUṣfūr, I, 368, Ibn Manẓūr, III, 1934, 1979, V, 3414, Howell, IV, fasc. I, 1297, Åkesson, *Ibn Masᶜūd* 362: (358):

> *"ᵓIḏā mā ᶜudda ᵓarbaᶜatun fisālun*
> *fa-zawǧuki ḫāmisun wa-ᵓabūki sādī".*
> "Whenever four mean unmanly fellows are
> reckoned,
> your husband is fifth, and your father sixth".

2.1.8.10. The substitution of the y for the t:

The *y* in *l-ṯāl(i)y* (that results after the assimilation of the *y* to the *i* in *l-ṯāl(i)ī)* is substituted for the *ṯ* of the base form *l-ṯāliṯ* "the third" (cf. Åkesson, *Ibn Masᶜūd* 332: fol. 35a, Nöldeke, *Grammatik* 13). The reason of this substitution seems to be the influence of the kasra preceding the *ṯ* (cf. Åkesson, *Ibn Masᶜūd* 332: fol. 35a). The example *l-ṯālī* occurs in these verses said by an unknown poet, cited by Rāzī in Ḫalīl b. Aḥmad ..., *Ḥurūf* 155, Ibn Ǧinnī, *Sirr II,* 764, Zamaḫšarī, 174, Ibn Yaᶜīš, X, 28, *Mulūkī* 255, Ibn ᶜUṣfūr, I, 378, Ibn Manẓūr, I, 497, Howell, IV, fasc. I, 1297-1298, Åkesson, *Ibn Masᶜūd* 362: (359):

"Yufdīka yā Zurᶜa ᵓabī wa-ḫālī
qad marra yawmāni wa-hāḏa l-ṯālī
wa-ᵓanta bi-l-hiğrāni lā tubālī".
"My father and my maternal uncle shall be a
ransom for you, O Zurᶜa!
Two days have passed and this is the third; and
you do not care for the desertion".

2.1.9. The substitution of the *w*

The *w* or the *ū* can be substituted for the following segments: 1- the *ā,* 2- the *y,* and 3- the *ᵓ*.

2.1.9.1. The substitution of the w for the ā:

The *w* in *ḍawāribu* "striking /pl." is necessarily substituted for the *ā* (cf. Ibn Ğinnī, *de Flexione* 24, *Sirr II,* 581-582, Zamaḫšarī, 174, Ibn Yaᶜīš, X, 29, Åkesson, *Ibn Masᶜūd* 334: fol. 35a). The example *ḍawāribu* is the broken pl. of the active participle *ḍāribun* and is conformable to the pattern *fawāᶜilu.* It is assumed that in its base form, the alif that marks the pl. is infixed after the infixed alif of the active participle *ḍāribun* causing a cluster of two vowelless alifs, namely *ḍ(a)āāribun.*

The 1st *ā* is substituted by the *w* to prevent this cluster so that it became *ḍawāribu.* The substitution of the *w* for the *ā* is considered as natural as they are both glides (cf. Åkesson, *Ibn Mas*ᶜ*ūd* 334: fol. 35a).

2.1.9.2. The substitution of the w for the y:

The *w* in the active participle Form IV *muwqinun* (that results after the assimilation of the *w* to the *u* in *m(u)ūqinun)* is necessarily substituted for the 1st radical vowelless *y* of the base form *muyqinun* "to be certain" (cf. Sībawaihi, II, 342, Ibn Ǧinnī, *de Flexione* 24, *Sirr II,* 584, Zamaḫšarī, 174, Ibn Yaᶜīš, X, 30, Åkesson, *Ibn Mas*ᶜ*ūd* 334: fol. 35a, Howell, IV, fasc. I, 1301) from *ᵓayqana* "was certain" with 1st radical *y*. The reason of this substitution is that the vowelless *y* is preceded by a ḍamma (cf. Åkesson, *Ibn Mas*ᶜ*ūd* 334: fol. 35a). A similar case is the active participle Form IV *muwsirun* > *m(u)ūsirun* from *ᵓaysara* "was prosperous", underlyingly *muysirun* "to be well off", in which the 1st radical vowelless *y* is also substituted by the *w* because it is preceded by a ḍamma (cf. Åkesson, *Complexity* par. 5.4.1.1., par. 9.1.5.).

Another example is the verb in the imperfect Form IV *yuwsiru* "is well off" > *y(u)ūsiru* underlyingly *yuysiru* of which the 1st vowelless radical *y* is changed into a *w* on account of the influence of the ḍamma preceding it (cf. Åkesson, *Complexity* par. 5.4.1.1.).

2.1.9.3. The substitution of the w for the hamza:

The *w* in *luwmun* (that results after the assimilation of the *w* to the *u* in *l(u)ūmun)* is substituted for the ʾ of the base form *luʾmun* "blame" (cf. Åkesson, *Ibn Masʿūd* 334: fol. 35a, *Complexity* par. 4.1.2.1.: 2).

2.1.10. The substitution of the *m*

The *m* can be substituted for the following segments: 1- the *w*, 2- the *l*, 3- the *n* and 4- the *b*.

2.1.10.1. The substitution of the m for the w:

The *m* in *famun* is substituted for the *w* (cf. Zaǧǧāǧī, *Maǧālis* 327, Ibn Ǧinnī, *Sirr I,* 413-421, Zamaḫšarī, 174, Ibn Yaʿīš, X, 33-34, Åkesson, *Ibn Masʿūd* 334: fol. 35a, Wright, II, 173, Vernier, I, 16-17) of the base form *fawahun* "mouth" of which the *h* is elided for the purpose of alleviation. According to

Sībawaihi, II, 342, the substitution of the *m* for the *w* in *famun* is rare.

2.1.10.2. The substitution of the m for the l:

The *m* in *ʾam* is substituted for the *l* of the definite article *ʾal*. *ʾam* denotes determination in the dialect of Ṭayyī and Ḥimyar which is named *al-ṭumṭumānīyatu* (cf. Rabin, 49). The tradition *laysa mina l-barri l-ṣiyāmu fī l-safari* "fasting in travelling is not an act of piety" has been said with the substitution of the *m* for the *l*, namely *laysa mina m-barri m-ṣiyāmu fī m-safari* by al-Namir b. Tawlab. It is cited by Ibn Ǧinnī, *Sirr I*, 423, Zamaḫšarī, 153, 174, Ibn Yaᶜīš, X, 34, Ibn Hišām, *Muġnī I*, 48, Ibn ᶜUṣfūr, I, 394, Ḥarīrī, *Durra* 183, Åkesson, *Ibn Masᶜūd* 334: fol. 35a-35b, Howell, II-III, 676, IV, fasc. I, 1330, Rabin, 36, Wright, II, 270, Carter, *Linguistics [Širbīnī, Āǧurrūmīya]* 22, 23. According to Ibn Masᶜūd (Åkesson, *Ibn Masᶜūd* 334: fol. 35b), this substitution of the *m* for the *l* is carried out on account of both these segments' common character in being among the voiced segments (for the segments' characters see par. 1.2.2.).

2.1.10.3. The substitution of the m for the n:

The *m* in *ᶜambarun* is substituted for the vowelless *n* of the base form *ᶜanbarun* "a warehouse" (cf. Sībawaihi, II, 342, Ibn Ǧinnī, *de Flexione* 26, Zamaḫšarī, 174-175, Ibn Yaᶜīš, X, 33-36, Åkesson, *Ibn Masᶜūd* 58: fol. 6 b, 334: fol. 35b). The substitution of the *m* for the *n* is necessary when the *n* occurs vowelless before the *b* because of the heaviness implied by the combination of the nasal *n* and the rigid *b.* Another example is *šambāʾun* said instead of *šanbāʾun* "having sharp canine teeth".

An example in which this substitution is carried out without that the *n* that precedes the *b* is vowelless is *banām* in which the *m* is substituted anomalously for the vowelled *n* of the base form *banān* "henna" (cf. Nöldeke, *Grammatik* 12). The example *l-banāmi* occurs in this verse said by al-ᶜAǧǧāǧ in the beginning of a poem in which he is praising Maslama b. ᶜAbd al-Malik. It is cited by Rāzī in Ḫalīl b. Aḥmad ..., *Ḥurūf* 154, Ibn Ǧinnī, *Sirr I,* 422, Zamaḫšarī, 174-175, Ibn Yaᶜīš, X, 33, 35, Ibn ᶜUṣfūr, I, 392, Howell, IV, fasc. I, 1332, Åkesson, *Ibn Masᶜūd* 366: (366):

"Yā Hāla ḏāta l-manṭiqi l-tamtāmi
wa-kaffiki l-muḫaḍḍabi l-banāmi".
"O Hāla [sc. name of a woman], possessed of the

lisping speech, and of your hand dyed in [the tips of] the fingers with henna".

<u>*2.1.10.4. The substitution of the m for the b:*</u>

The *m* in *rātiman* is substituted for the *b* of the base form *rātiban* (cf. Zamaḫšarī, 175, Ibn Ya^cīš, X, 35) in the sentence *mā ẓiltu rātiman* "I have not ceased to be constant" (cf. Åkesson, *Ibn Mas^cūd* 334: fol. 35b). The reason of this substitution is the oneness of both these segments' point of articulation on account that they are both labials (for the segments see par. 1.2.1.).

2.1.11. The substitution of the ṣ

The *ṣ* can be substituted for the *s*.

<u>*2.1.11.1. The substitution of the ṣ for the*</u> *s*

An example is *ʾaṣbaġa* in which the *ṣ* is allowably substituted for the *s* of its base form *ʾasbaġa* "to make flow in exceeding measure" (cf. Zamaḫšarī, 176, Ibn Ya^cīš, X, 51-52, Howell, IV, fasc. I, 1378-1380, Fleisch, *Traité I,* 80-81). It occurs in the sur. 31: 20 *(wa-ʾaṣbaġa ᶜalaykum niᶜamahu)* "And has made His bounties flow to you in exceeding measure", underlyingly *wa-ʾasbaġa,* read with both the *s* and the *ṣ* (cf. Ibn Ǧinnī, *Sirr I,* 212). The reason of this substitution is the proximity of the points of articulation of both the *s* and the *ṣ* (cf. Åkesson, *Ibn Masᶜūd* 334: fol. 35b), on account that they both originate from the part which is between the tip of the tongue and the tops of the two upper central incissors and are dentals (for the segments see par. 1.2.1).

2.1.12. The substitution of the *ā*

The *ā* can be substituted for the following segments: 1- the *w,* 2- the *y* and 3- the *ʾ*.

2.1.12.1. The substitution of the ā for the w:

An example is *q(a)āla* in which the *ā* is necessarily substituted for the *w* of the base form *qawala* "to say" (cf. Åkesson, *Ibn Masᶜūd* 334: fol. 35b). The reason of this substitution is that the vowelled *w* is found in a measure of a verbal form, namely *faᶜala,* and is preceded by a fatḥa (cf. Åkesson, *Complexity* par. 6.5.1.1.: 1, par. 9.1.2.1.).

2.1.12.2. The substitution of the ā for the y:

An example is *b(a)āᶜa* in which the *ā* is necessarily substituted for the *y* of the base form *bayaᶜa* "to sell" (cf. ibid). The reason of this substitution is that the vowelled *y* is found in a measure of a verbal form, namely *faᶜala,* and is preceded by a fatḥa (cf. Åkesson, *Complexity* par. 6.5.1.2.: 1, par. 9.1.2.1.).

2.1.12.3. The substitution of the ā for the hamza:

An example is *r(a)āsun* in which the *ā* is allowably substituted for the ᵓ of the base form *raᵓsun* "head" (cf. Åkesson, *Ibn Masᶜūd* 334: fol. 35b, Nöldeke, *Grammatik* 6). The reason of this change is the vowellessness of the ᵓ and the vowelling of the segment preceding it (see Åkesson, *Complexity* par. 4.1.2.1.: 1).

2.1.13. The substitution of the *l*

The *l* can be substituted for the following segments: 1- the *n* and 2- the *ḍ*.

2.1.13.1. The substitution of the l for the n:

An example is *ʾuṣaylālun* in which the *l* is substituted for the *n* of the base form *ʾuṣaylānun* "evening" (cf. Åkesson, *Ibn Masʿūd* 334: fol. 35b, Wright, II, 175). The example *ʾuṣaylālan* occurs in this verse said by al-Nābiġa al-Ḏubyānī praising al-Nuʿmān b. al-Munḏir, cited by Rāzī in Ḫalīl b. Aḥmad ..., *Ḥurūf* 1538, Ibn Ğinnī, *Lumaʿ* 28, Muʾaddib, *Taṣrif* 338, Ibn al-Sarrāğ, *Uṣūl III,* 275, Zamaḫšarī, 176, Ibn Yaʿīš, *Mulūkī* 106, 216, Ibn al-Anbārī, *Inṣāf* Q. 19, 79, Howell, IV, fasc. I, 1367, Åkesson, *Ibn Masʿūd* 368: (370):

"Waqaftu fīhā ʾuṣaylālan ʾusāʾiluhā
ʿayyat ğawāban wa-mā bi-l-rabʿi min ʿaḥad.
"I stopped in it a short time at evening, questioning
it [about its inmates]:
it was unable to answer, nor was any one in the
abode".

2.1.13.2. The substitution of the l for the ḍ:

An example is *ʾilṭağaʿa* in which the *l* is substituted for the *ḍ* of the base form *ʾiḍṭağaʿa* "to lay down to sleep" (cf. Åkesson, *Ibn Masʿūd* 334: fol. 35b). The example *fa-lṭağaʿ* is found in this verse said by Manẓūr b. Murṯid al-Asadī (cf. Fischer/

Braūnlich, *Šawāhid* 134) describing a wolf that meant to catch a gazelle. It is cited by Ibn Ǧinnī, *Sirr I,* 321, *Ḫaṣā'iṣ I,* 63, 263, III, 163, Zamaḫšarī, 176, Ibn Yaᶜīš, IX, 82, X, 46, *Mulūkī* 216, Ibn ᶜAqīl, II, 548, Ibn ᶜUṣfūr, I, 403, Suyūṭī, *Ašbāh I,* 601, Ibn Manẓūr, IV, 2554, Howell, IV, fasc. I, 848, 1368, Åkesson, *Ibn Masᶜūd* 368: (371):

> *"Lammā ra'ā 'an lā daᶜah wa-lā šibaᶜ*
> *māla 'ilā 'arṭāti ḫiqfin fa-lṭaǧaᶜ".*
> "When he [sc. the wolf] saw that there was no
> ease, and no glutting of his appetite [in the pursuit
> of the gazelle],
> he turned aside to an Arṭā tree of a curving tract of
> sand, and lay down to sleep".

2.1.14. The substitution of the *z*

The *z* can be substituted for the following segments: 1- the *s* and 2- the *ṣ*.

2.1.14.1. The substitution of the z for the s:

An example is *yazdulu* in which the *z* is substituted for the *s* of the base form *yasdulu* "he losens (his garment)" (cf. Ibn

Ǧinnī, *Sirr I,* 196, Zamaḫšarī, 177, Ibn Yaᶜīš, X, 52, Ibn Manẓūr, III, 2036, Åkesson, *Ibn Masᶜūd* 334: fol. 35b, Howell, IV, fasc. I, 1381).

2.1.14.2. The substitution of the z for the ṣ:

An example is *fazdī* in which the *z* is substituted for the *ṣ* of the base form *faṣdī* "my way of bleeding". This substitution is carried out when the *z* is vowelless and occurs before a *d*. The example *fazdī* occurs in this phrase said by Ḥatim when he had slaughtered a she-camel for a guest and he was asked: "Why did you not bleed her?", and he answered: *hākaḏā fazdī ʾanah* "This is my way of bleeding, mine" (cf. Zaǧǧāǧī, *Maǧālis* 136, Zamaḫšarī, 177, Ibn Yaᶜīš, X, 52, Åkesson, *Ibn Masᶜūd* 334: fol. 35b, Howell, IV, fasc. I, 856, 1383), with this substitution taking place in *faṣdī* resulting in *fazdī.*

2.1.15. The substitution of the *ṭ*

The *ṭ* can be substituted for the *t*.

2.1.15.1. The substitution of the ṭ for the t:

This substitution is necessary if the *t* follows one of the segments of covering, namely the *ṣ, ḍ, ṭ* and *ẓ* (for the segments' characters see par. 1.2.2.). This occurs in two cases:

- In Form VIII *ʾiftaʿala* in which the 1st radical is a segment of covering, e.g. Form VIII *ʾiṣṭabara* in which the *ṭ* is necessarily substituted for the infixed *t* of the base form *ʾiṣtabara* "to have patience" (cf. Åkesson, *Ibn Masʿūd* 334: fol. 35b and this study par. 1.4.1.1.3.2.: 4), *ʾiḍṭaraba* underlyingly *ʾiḍtaraba* "to be in a state of agitation" (cf. par. 1.4.1.1.3.2.: 5), *ʾiṭṭalaba* originaly *ʾiṭtalaba* "to seek" (cf. par. 1.4.1.1.3.2.: 6), and *ʾiẓṭalama* "to put with wrong" underlyingly *ʾiẓtalama* (cf. par. 1.4.1.1.3.2.: 7).

- In some cases of verbs in the perfect of which the 3rd radical is one of the segments of covering, to which the agent pronoun of the 1st or of the 2nd person of the perfect, namely the *-tu* or the *-ta* respectively, is suffixed to, e.g. *faḥaṣṭu* in which the *ṭ* is substituted for the *t* which is the suffixed agent pronoun of the 1st person of the sing. of *faḥaṣtu* "I scraped a hollow" (cf. Sībawaihi, II, 341, Ibn Ǧinnī, *Sirr I,* 219-220, Zamaḫšarī, 176, Ibn Yaʿīš, X, 46-48, Ibn ʿUṣfūr, I, 360-361, Åkesson, *Ibn Masʿūd* 334: fol. 35b, Howell, IV, fasc. I, 1369-1370, Vernier, I, 356).

Other examples are *ḥafiẓṭu* and *ḥafiẓṭa* said instead of *ḥafiẓtu* "I kept" and *ḥafiẓta* "you kept" respectively and *ḥuṣṭu* and *ḥuṣṭa* said instead of *ḥuṣtu* "I sealed" and *ḥuṣta* "you sealed" respectively.

3. BIBLIOGRAPHY

3.1. Primary sources

ᶜAbd al-Ḥamīd, *Taṣrīf* = ᶜAbd al-Ḥamīd, M. Muḥyī l-Dīn, *Takmila fī Taṣrīf al-afᶜāl,* the work printed after Ibn ᶜAqīl, *Šarḥ II.*

Åkesson, *Ibn Masᶜūd* = Åkesson, J. , *Arabic Morphology and Phonology based on the Marāḥ al-arwāḥ by Aḥmad b. ᶜAlī b. Masᶜūd, Presented with an Introduction, Arabic Edition, English Translation and Commentary,* Leiden 2001.

Bakkūš, *Taṣrif* = Al-Bakkūš, Ṭ., *al-Taṣrif al-ᶜarabī,* Tunis 1973.

Carter, *Linguistics [Širbīnī, Āǧurrūmīya]* = Carter, M. G., *Arab Linguistics, an introductory classical text with translation and notes,* Amsterdam 1981.

Daqr, *Mu^c^ğam* = Daqr, ^c^Abd al-Ġanī, *Mu^c^ğam al-naḥw,* Beirut 1407 A.H. /1986.

Ḫalīl b. Aḥmad..., *Ḥurūf* = Ḫalīl b. Aḥmad wa-b. al-Sakīt wa-l-Rāzī, *Ṯalāṯat kutub fī l-ḥurūf,* Ed. R. ^c^Abd al-Tawwāb, Cairo 1982.

Ḥarīrī, *Durra* = Al-Ḥarîrî, Abū Muḥammad al-Qāsim b. ^c^Alī, *Durrat al-ġawwâṣ,* Ed. H. Thorbecke, Leipzig 1871.

Ibn al-Anbārī, *Inṣāf* = Ibn al-Anbārī, Abū l-Barakāt, *Kitāb al-inṣāf fī masā^ʾ^il al-ḫilāf bayna l-naḥwīyīn al-baṣrīyīn wa-l-kūfīyīn: Die grammatischen Schulen von Kufa und Basra,* Ed. G. Weil, Leiden 1913.

Ibn ^c^Aqīl = Ibn ^c^Aqīl, *Bihā^ʾ^ al-Dīn ^c^Abdallāh, ˇŠarḥ ^c^alā alfīyat Ibn Mālik,* Ed. ^c^A. al-Ḥamīd, 2 vol., undated.

Ibn Fāris, *Ṣāḥibī* = Ibn Fāris, Aḥmad, *al-Ṣāḥibī fī fiqh al-luġa wa-sanan al-^c^arab fī kalāmihā,* Ed. M. al-Chouémi, (bibliotheca Philologica; I), Beyrouth 1382/1963.

Ibn Ǧinnī, *de Flexione* = Ibn Ǧinnîi, Abū l-Fatḥ ^c^Uṯmān, *de Flexione Libellvs,* Ed. G. Hoberg, Lipsiae, 1885.

Ibn Ǧinnī, *Ḫaṣā^ʾ^iṣ* = Ibn Ǧinnī, Abū l-Fatḥ ^c^Uṯmān, *al-Ḫaṣā^ʾ^iṣ,* Ed. M. A. al-Naǧǧār, 3 vol., Cairo 1371/1952-1376/1956.

Ibn Ǧinnī, *Luma*ᶜ = Ibn Ǧinnī, Abū l-Fatḥ ᶜUṯmān, *Kitāb al-lumaᶜ fi-n-naḥw,* Ed. H. M. Kechrida, Uppsala 1976.

Ibn Ǧinnī, *Munṣif* = Ibn Ǧinnī, Abū l-Fatḥ ᶜUṯmān, *al-Munṣif fī šarḥ taṣrīf al-Māzinī,* Ed. I. Muṣṭafā, ᶜA. Amīn, 3 vol., Cairo 1373/1954-1379/1960.

Ibn Ǧinnī, *Sirr* = Ibn Ǧinnī, Abū l-Fatḥ ᶜUṯmān, *Sirr ṣināᶜat al-iᶜrāb,* Ed. Ḥ. Hindāwī, 2 vol., Damascus 1405/1985.

Ibn Ḫālawaihi, *Qirāʾāt* = Ibn Ḫālawaihi, Abū ᶜAbd Allāh al-Ḥusain b. Aḥmad, *Iᶜrāb al-qirāʾāt al-sabᶜ wa-ᶜilaluhā,* Ed. ᶜAbd al-Raḥmān b. Sulaimān al-ᶜAtīmain, 2 vol., Cairo 1413/1992.

Ibn Hišām, *Muġnī* = Ibn Hišām, Ǧamāl al-Dīn Abū Muḥammad ᶜAbdallāh b. Yūsuf, *Muġnī l-labīb ᶜan kutub al-aᶜārīb,* 2 vol., Ed. M. Mubārak and M. ᶜA. Ḥ. Allāh, Beirut 1972.

Ibn Mālik, *La Alfiya* = Ibn Mālik, Muḥammad b. ᶜAbd Allāh, *La ʾAlfiyyah d'Ibnu-Malik* [pp. 1-227], suivie de (->) *La Lāmiyyah* du meme auteur (pp. 228-353) avec traduction et notes en français et un lexique des termes techniques par A. Goguyer, Beyrouth 1888.

Ibn Manẓūr = Ibn Manẓūr, Ǧamāl al-Dīn, *Lisān al-ᶜArab,* 6 vol., Beirut undated.

Ibn Muǧāhid, *Sabʿa* = Ibn Muǧāhid, Abū Bakr Aḥmad b. Mūsā, *al-Sabʿa fī l-qirāʾāt,* Ed. Š. Ḍaif, Cairo 1972.

Ibn al-Sarrāǧ, *ʾUṣūl* = Ibn al-Sarrāǧ, Abū Bakr, *al-ʾUṣūl fī l-Naḥw,* Ed. ʿA. Ḥ. al-Fatlī, Beirut 1408/1988.

Ibn ʿUṣfūr = Ibn ʿUṣfūr al-Ašbīlī, Abū l-ʿAbbās ʿAlī b. Muʾmin, *al-Mumtiʿ fī l-taṣrīf,* Ed. F. al-Dīn Qabāwih, Aleppo 1390/1970.

Ibn Yaʿīš = Ibn Yaʿīš, Muwaffaq al-Dīn Abū l-Barāʾ Yaʿīš, *Šarḥ al-mufaṣṣal, 2* vol., Beirut undated.

Ibn Yaʿīš, *Mulūkī* = Ibn Yaʿīš, Muwaffaq al-Dīn Abū l-Barāʾ Yaʿīš, *Šarḥ al-mulūkī fī l-taṣrīf,* Ed. Faḫr al-Dīn Qabāwa, Aleppo 1393/1973.

Kuṯayyir, *Dīwān* = Kuṯayyir ʿIzza, *Dīwān,* Ed. I. ʿAbbās, Beirut 1391/1971.

Muʾaddib, *Taṣrīf* = Al-Muʾaddib, al-Qāsim b. Muḥammad b. Saʿīd, *Daqāʾiq al-taṣrīf,* Ed. A. N. al-Qaisī, Ḥ. Ṣ. al-Ḍāmin and Ḥ. Tūrāl, Iraq 1407/1987.

Sībawaihi = Sîbawaihi, Abū Bišr ʿAmr b. ʿUṯmān, *Le Livre de Sîbawaihi (Kitāb Sībawaihi), Traité de grammaire arabe,* Ed. H. Derenbourg, 2 vol., Paris 1881-1889. Réimpression: 1970.

Širbīnī, *Āǧurrūmīya* = see Carter, *Linguistics.*

Suyūṭī, *Ašbāh* = Al-Suyūtī, Ǧalāl al-Dīn Abū l-Faḍl ᶜAbd al-Raḥmān, *al-ᵓAšbāh wa-l-naẓāᵓir,* Ed. ᶜAbd AIlāh Nabhān, 4 vol., Damascus 1406/1985.

Versteegh, *Zaǧǧāǧī* = Versteegh, K., *The explanation of linguistic causes. Az-Zaǧǧāǧī's theory of grammar. Introduction, translation, commentary,* Amsterdam 1995.

Zaǧǧāǧī, *Maǧālis* = Al-Zaǧǧāǧī, Abū Qāsim ᶜAbd al-Raḥmān, *Maǧālis al-ᶜulamāᵓ*, Ed. ᶜA. S. M. Harūn, Kuwait 1962.

Zamaḫšarī = Zamaḫsᵓario, Abū l-Qāsim Maḥmūd b. ᶜUmar, *al-Mufaṣṣal,* Ed. J. P. Broch, Christianiae 1840.

3.2. Secondary sources

ᶜAbd al-Tawwāb, *Taṭawwur* = ᶜAbd al-Tawwāb, Ramaḍān, *al-Taṭawwur al-luġawī, maẓāhiruhu wa-ᶜilaluhu wa-qawānīnuhu,* Cairo 1404/1983.

Åkesson, *Complexity* = Åkesson, J., *The Complexity of the Irregular Verbal and Nominal Forms & the Phonological Changes in Arabic,* Lund 2009.

Åkesson, *Ibn Masᶜūd* = Åkesson, J., *Arabic Morphology and Phonology based on the Marāḥ al-arwāḥ by Aḥmad b. ᶜAlī b. Masᶜūd, Presented with an Introduction, Arabic Edition, English Translation and Commentary,* Leiden 2001.

Cantineau, *Études* = Cantineau, J., *Études de linguistique arabe,* Memorial Jean Cantineau, Paris 1960.

Cantineau, *Voyelle* = Cantineau, J., *La Voyelle de secours dans les langues sémitiques,* in: Semitica II, 1949.

Carter, *Linguistics* [Širbīnī, *Āğurrūmīya]* = Carter, M. G., *Arab Linguistics, an introductory classical text with translation and notes,* Amsterdam 1981.

Fischer/Braūnlich, *Šawāhid* = Fischer, A. und Bräunlich, E., Schawāhid-Indices, *Indices der Reimwörter und der Dichter der in den arabischen Schawāhid-Kommentaren und in verwandten Werken erläuterten Belegverse,* Leipzig und Wien, 1945.

Fleisch, *Arabe* = Fleish, H., *L'arabe classique, Esquisse d'une structure linguistique,* Beyrouth 1968.

Fleisch, *Traité I* = Fleisch, H., *Traité de Philologie Arabe, vol. I, Préliminaires, Phonétique Morphologie Nominale,* Beyrouth 1961.

Fleisch, *Traité II* = Fleisch, H., *Traité de Philologie Arabe, vol. II, Pronoms, Morphologie verbale, Particules,* Beyrouth 1979.

Howell = Howell, M. S., *Grammar of the Classical Arabic Language,* 4 parts in 7 vol., Allahabad 1880-1911.

Lane = Lane, E.W., *Arabic-English Lexicon,* 8 in 2 vol., London 1863-1893. Reprint: 1984.

Mokhlis, *Taṣrīf* = Mokhlis, H., *Théorie du Taṣrīf et traitement du lexique chez les grammairiens arabes,* Germany 1997.

Nöldeke, *Grammatik* = Nöldeke, T., *Zur Grammatik des Classischen Arabisch im Anhang: Die Handschriftlichen ergänzungen in dem Handexemplar Theodor Nöldekes bearbeitet und mit zuzätzen versehen von Anton Spitaler,* Darmstadt 1963.

Penrice, *Dictionary* = Penrice, J., *A Dictionary and Glossary of the Kor-ân,* London 1873. Reprint: 1971.

Rabin = Rabin, C., *Ancient West-Arabian,* London 1951.

Roman, *Étude* = Roman, A., *Étude de la phonologie et de la morphologie de la koinè arabe,* 2 vol., Publications de l'Université de Provence, Marseille 1983.

De Sacy = De Sacy, S., *Grammaire arabe,* 2 vol., Tunis 1904-1905.

Talmon, *ᶜAyn* = Talmon, R., *Arabic Grammar in its formative Age, Kitāb al-ᶜAyn and its Attribution to Ḫalīl b. Aḥmad,* Leiden - New York - Køln 1997.

Vernier = Vernier, D., *Grammaire arabe,* 2 vol., Beyrouth 1891.

Versteegh, *Langage* = Versteegh, C. H. M., *The Arabic language,* Edinburgh 1996.

Versteegh, *Zağğāğī* = Versteegh, K., *The explanation of linguistic causes. Az-Zağğāğī's theory of grammar. Introduction, translation, commentary,* Amsterdam 1995.

Vollers, *Volkssprache* = Vollers, K., *Volkssprache und Schriftsprache im alten Arabien,* Strassburg 1906.

Wright = Wright, W., *A Grammar of the Arabic Language,* Cambridge, Third Edition 1985.

4. INDEX OF QUR'ANIC QUOTATIONS

Sur.	v.	page
1:	2-3	19
2:	19	17
2:	72	49
2:	170	65
2:	213	18
2:	133	66
2:	235	17
2:	255	18
2:	269	49
2:	284	59

3:	85	18
3:	129	66
3:	147	63
3:	151	17
3:	185	62
4:	81	45, 61
4:	156	66
6:	25	43
6:	53	66
7:	77	17
7:	143	19
7:	167	66
8:	35	28
9:	38	48
9:	80	63
9:	99	18
10:	24	50
10:	35	55
11:	66	20

11:	78	63
16:	70	66
16:	91	62
19:	2	18
19:	4	64
19:	29	63
20:	33	19
20:	35	19
20:	97	24
22:	36	60
22:	65	63
24:	45	64
24:	62	64
25:	43	19
27:	47	53
29:	26	66
31:	20	101
33:	10	63
33:	33	25

34:	9	64
36:	49	57
37:	8	43, 51
41:	50	63
47:	18	65
48:	29	62
51:	1	60
56:	65	24
61:	12	63
70:	3-4	61
71:	16	64
80:	3-4	49
89:	6	65
89:	19	77

5. INDEX OF VERSES

Ḫālī ᶜUwayfun wa-ᵓAbū ᶜAliǧǧi 83

Huwa l-ǧawādu l-laḏī yuᶜṭīka nāᶜilahu 42

ᵓIḏā l-kirāmu btadarū l-bāᶜa badar 27

ᵓIḏā mā ᶜudda ᵓarbaᶜatun fisālun 94

La-hā ᵓašārīru min laḥmin tutammiruhu 93

Lāhumma ᵓin kunta qabilta ḥaǧǧatiǧ 82

Nazūru mraᵓan ᵓammā l-ᵓilāha fa-yattaqī 27

Qāmat bi-hā tanšudu kullu l-munšadi 92

Ṣafqatu ḏī ḏaᶜālitin samūli 81

Wa-baldatin qāliṣatin ᵓamwāᵓuhā 75

Wa-hayyağa l-ḥayya min dārin fa-ẓalla lahum 85

Wa-kunnā ḥasibnāhum fawārisa kahmasi 14

Wa-māğa sāᶜātin malā l-wadīqi 76

Wa-mā maliltu wa-lākin zāda ḥubbukum 25

Wa-manhalin laysa lahu ḥawāziqu 91

Waqaftu fīhā ᵓuṣaylālan ᵓusāᵓiluhā 103

Yā dāra Mayya bi-l-dakādīki l-buraq 75

Yā Hāla ḏāta l-manṭiqi l-tamtāmi 99

Yā qātala l-lāhu banī l-siᶜlāti 79

Yufdīka yā Zurᶜa ᵓabī wa-ḫālī 95

Ẓiltu fīhā ḏāta yawma wāqifan 25

6. INDEX OF NAMES

ᶜAbd al-ᶜAzīz b. Marwān 27
ᶜAbd al-Ḥamīd 24, 25
ᶜAbd al-Tawwāb 37, 46, 69, 78
Abū ᶜAmr 17, 18, 19, 20, 55, 57, 61, 62, 63, 64, 66
Abū Bakr 57
Abū Bakr b. Muǧāhid 63
Abū Ǧaᶜfar 57
Abū Zaid: Saᶜīd b. Aus b. Ṯābit al-Anṣārī 82
Al-ᶜAǧǧāǧ 26, 99
Åkesson 5, 6, 8, 12, 13, 14, 15, 23, 24, 25, 26, 31, 32, 33, 34, 35, 37, 38, 39, 40, 41, 42, 43, 44, 46, 48, 52, 53, 55, 58, 62, 68, 69, 70, 71, 72, 73, 74, 75, 76, 77, 78, 79, 80, 82, 83, 84, 85, 86, 88, 89, 90, 91, 92, 93, 94, 95, 96, 97, 98, 99, 100, 101, 102, 103, 104, 105, 106

Al-Aᶜmaš 57
Al-Aᶜrağ 57
ᶜĀṣim 26, 57
Baiḍāwī 57
Bakkūš 29, 35, 36
Banū ᶜĀmir 24
Banū ᶜAwf b. Saᶜd 80
Banū Bakr b. Waᵓīl 85
Banū Saᶜd 83
Banū Tamīm 14, 23, 78, 83
Braūnlich 42, 103
Cantineau 45, 57, 59, 60, 61
Carter 98
Dakwān 57
Daqir 78
Fischer 42, 103
Fleisch 15, 32, 33, 57, 59, 69, 86, 100
Ḫalaf al-Aḥmar 91
Ḫalīl b. Aḥmad 70, 79, 86, 94, 99, 103
Ḥamza 57, 60
Harim b. Sinān 42
Ḥarīrī 98
Al-Ḥasan al-Baṣrī 57
Ḥātim 105
Ḥiğāzīs 24, 78

Ḥimyār 98
Hišām 57
Howell 5, 6, 10, 11, 12, 13, 14, 18, 24, 27, 31, 32, 41, 42, 48, 49, 50, 51, 52, 53, 55, 60, 61, 68, 69, 70, 71, 72, 73, 74, 75, 76, 78, 79, 80, 81, 82, 83, 84, 85, 86, 88, 89, 90, 91, 92, 93, 94, 96, 98, 99, 100, 103, 104, 105, 106
Ibn ᶜAlāᵓ 60
Ibn al-Anbārī 103
Ibn ᶜAqīl 13, 24, 25, 26, 35, 37, 69, 104
Ibn Fāris 79, 83, 84,
Ibn Ǧinnī 26, 27, 41, 42, 68, 70, 71, 73, 74, 75, 79, 80, 81, 82, 83, 86, 88, 89, 91, 92, 93, 94, 95, 96, 97, 98, 99, 101, 103, 104, 105, 106
Ibn Ḫālawaihi 58
Ibn Hišām 98
Ibn Kaṯīr 57
Ibn Mālik 24
Ibn Manẓūr 13, 14, 25, 33, 44, 57, 70, 72, 73, 74, 75, 79, 80, 85, 90, 91, 92, 94, 104, 105
Ibn Masᶜūd 5, 6, 8, 12, 13, 14, 15, 23, 24, 25, 26, 31, 32, 33, 34, 35, 37, 38, 39, 40, 41, 42, 43, 44, 46, 48, 52, 53, 55, 58, 62, 68, 69, 70, 71, 72, 73, 74, 75, 76, 77, 78, 79, 80, 82, 83, 84, 85, 86, 88, 89, 90, 91, 92, 93, 94, 95, 96, 97, 98, 99, 100, 101, 102, 103, 104, 105, 106
Ibn Muǧāhid 58
Ibn al-Sarrāǧ 82, 93, 103

Ibn ᶜUṣfūr 17, 18, 19, 20, 27, 61, 62, 63, 64, 65, 66, 68, 69, 70, 71, 72, 73, 74, 76, 78, 79, 81, 82, 83, 91, 92, 93, 94, 98, 99, 104, 106

Ibn Yaᶜīš 14, 17, 18, 19, 26, 27, 40, 41, 42, 60, 61, 62, 63, 64, 65, 66, 68, 69, 70, 71, 72, 73, 74, 76, 77, 78, 79, 80, 81, 82, 83, 84, 85, 86, 88, 90, 91, 92, 93, 94, 95, 96, 97, 98, 99, 100, 103, 104, 105, 106

ᶜIlbāᵓ b. Arqam al-Yaškarī 79

Imruᵓu l-Qais 94

Kaᶜb 11

Kahmas 14

Al-Kisāᵓī 57, 65

Kuṯayyir 27

Lane 15, 32, 33, 34, 36, 37, 41, 48, 49, 50, 51, 52, 82, 83

Manẓūr b. Murṯid al-Asadī 103

Maslama b. ᶜAbd al-Malik 99

Al-Māzinī 72

Mokhlis 71, 73,

Muᵓaddib 26, 42, 57, 103

Muḥammad 70

Al-Nābiġa al-Ḏubyānī 103

Nāfiᶜ 26, 55

Al-Namir b. Tawlab 98

Numair 11

al-Nuᶜmān b. al-Munḏir 103

Nöldeke 91, 93. 94, 99, 102

Penrice 25, 48, 49, 50, 52, 54
Qālūn 57
Rabin 98
Rāzī 70, 79, 86, 94, 99, 103
Roman 7, 26, 27, 59
De Sacy 13, 23, 24, 32, 34, 37, 39, 43, 46, 57, 85
Saᶜīd b. Aus b. Ṯābit al-Anṣārī 82
Sībawaihi 3, 5, 6, 9, 13, 14, 15, 16, 20, 24, 26, 27, 41, 42, 43, 59, 70, 71, 76, 78, 79, 83, 84, 85, 86, 91, 93, 96, 98, 99, 106
Širbīnī 98
Suyūṭī 104
Talmon 24
Tamīm 14, 23, 78, 83
Ṭayyī 98
ᶜUmar b. Abī Rabīᶜa 25
ᶜUmar b. Abī Rabīᶜa al-Maḫzūmi 24
Vernier 13, 30, 37, 38, 39, 41, 72, 82, 83, 85, 88, 97, 10
Versteegh 3, 85
Vollers 60, 61, 62, 63, 64, 65, 66
Warš 57
Wright 7, 13, 23, 24, 29, 31, 32, 33, 34, 37, 38, 39, 40, 41, 43, 46, 50, 53, 59, 85, 88, 91, 97, 98, 103
Yaᶜqūb al-Ḥaḍrami 63
Yemen 81
Yemenites 79

Zaǧǧāǧī 33, 85, 97, 105
Zamaḫšarī 5, 6, 7, 12, 13, 17, 18, 19, 26, 27, 34, 35, 37, 38, 39, 40, 41, 42, 43, 46, 59, 60, 61, 62, 63, 64, 65, 66, 68, 69, 70, 71, 72, 73, 74, 76, 78, 79, 80, 81, 82, 83, 84, 85, 86, 88, 90, 91, 93, 94, 95, 96, 97, 98, 99, 100, 103, 104, 105, 106
Zuhair b. Abī Sulmā al-Muzanī 42

www.ingramcontent.com/pod-product-compliance
Lightning Source LLC
Chambersburg PA
CBHW021004090426
42738CB00007B/650
* 9 7 8 9 1 9 7 7 6 4 1 6 2 *